ultimate

style

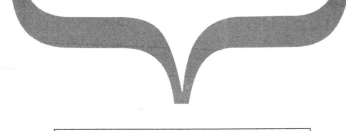

THE RULES OF WRITING

SPARK
NOTES

A BARNES & NOBLE PUBLICATION

WRITER: Emma Chastain
EDITORIAL DIRECTOR: Laurie Barnett
EDITOR: Anna Medvedovsky

DESIGN: Dan O. Williams
PRODUCTION EDITOR: Jessica Allen
PRODUCTION: Adrienne Craig-Williams, Dan Visel

Spark Educational Publishing
A Division of Barnes & Noble Publishing
120 Fifth Avenue
New York, NY 10011

ISBN 1-4114-0285-5

Please submit changes or report errors to www.sparknotes.com/errors.

Printed and bound in Canada.

Library of Congress Cataloging-in-Publication Data

Chastain, Emma, 1979–
  SparkNotes ultimate style / Emma Chastain.
    p. cm.
  ISBN 1-4114-0285-5
  1. Authorship–Style manuals. I. Title.

PN203.C459 2005
808'.027–dc22

2004022250

From the most clueless freshman to the most seasoned writer, everyone occasionally struggles with a grammatical issue. Maybe you have trouble remembering when to use *who* and when to use *whom*. Or maybe you find yourself thinking, is it "the donut *which* I just ate" or "the donut *that* I just ate"? When these kinds of questions pop up, you don't want to wade through a hefty, technical grammar manual or make wild-eyed guesses in the dark. You want succinct, easy-to-find answers. May we suggest *SparkNotes Ultimate Style*?

Unlike other manuals, which are organized by topic, *SparkNotes Ultimate Style* is organized alphabetically. You'll find the entry on *Wordiness* right next to the entry on *Who vs. Whom* and *Dashes* cheek by jowl with *Dates*. Finding the answer to your question is as easy as humming the alphabet.

You'll notice that some entries cover a gigantic subject (*Commas*). Others cover an extremely specific topic (*Circa*). This imbalance in the entries' breadth might surprise you, but we did it in the name of helpfulness: we wanted to cover those grammatical problems that cause the most angst and make it easy for you to find answers to your questions. So many people get *lie* and *lay* confused, for example, that we devoted an entire entry to the problem.

Language is a living, changing thing, and its guidelines are evolving all the time. We've put together a set of rules that are traditional but not stuffy or old-fashioned. You will undoubtedly disagree with some of them. For instance, we don't think ending sentences with prepositions is anything to get upset about. We stand firmly behind the recommendations we've made, but many of them are a matter of personal preference. If you loathe (or like!) our rules, let us know at www.sparknotes.com/comments. We'd love to hear from you.

ACCENTS

When using accented words from foreign languages, include the correct accents and put the words in italics.

✓ *l'opéra, niños, hüten*

Some foreign-language words, such as *cliché*, have become firmly entrenched in the language. If a word is in the dictionary, it is considered an English-language word and should not be italicized. You may choose to keep or drop the accents. SparkNotes prefers keeping the original accents, especially since contemporary word-processing software makes it so easy.

✓ His naïveté drives me crazy.

ALSO OK: His naivete drives me crazy.

✓ Her doppelgänger haunted her day and night.

ALSO OK: Her doppelganger haunted her day and night.

ACCEPT vs. EXCEPT

accept: to receive (*v.*)

✓ At the assembly, Ike accepted the award for best gym attendance.

except: aside from (*prep.*)

✓ No one except Ike enjoys dodgeball.

ACTIVE VOICE

Active voice refers to sentences where the subject performs the action of the verb instead of receiving it.

ACTIVE VOICE: The goth kids boycotted the prom.

The subject (*goth kids*) performs the action (*boycotted*).

PASSIVE VOICE: The prom was boycotted by the goth kids.

The subject (*prom*) receives the action (*boycotted*).

Although sentences in the passive voice are not grammatically incorrect, active voice is usually preferable. Active voice will make your writing specific, interesting, and muscular.

UNDESIRABLE: The morning announcements are always read by Mrs. Pringle.

DESIRABLE: Mrs. Pringle always reads the morning announcements.

Occasionally, you won't know who or what performed an action, and you'll have to use the passive voice.

✓ Leah's car was stolen in the dead of night.

A.D.

The abbreviation A.D. stands for the Latin *anno Domini* ("in the year of our lord"). It is used for years after 1 on our calendar. In practice, it is only used for years before about A.D. 1000 and to clarify potential ambiguities. It comes before the designated year.

We at SparkNotes prefer to use small capital letters and periods, but you may choose to use uppercase letters for simplicity and/or omit the periods.

✓ St. Augustine, the author of the *Confessions*, was born in A.D. 354.

Because not all people believe that the phrase *our lord* is appropriate, some writers prefer to use the abbreviation C.E., which stands for *common era* and comes after the designated year.

✓ St. Augustine was born in 354 C.E.

ADDRESSES

When mentioning an address in your writing, place commas after each section of the address.

✓ The biggest bully in fifth grade lives at 123 Snippet Drive, Boise, Idaho, 83701.

In a mailing address, place a comma between the city and the state only.

✓ Bully Maguire
123 Snippet Drive
Boise, ID 83701

ADJECTIVES

Adjectives describe or modify nouns.

✓ skinny, naturalistic, gloomy, pink, sparkling

Adjectives almost always precede nouns.

✓ the green grass; a haughty hostess; that finicky old cat

Adjectives may follow nouns for poetic or dramatic effect.

✓ The hostess, haughty and hirsute, led us to our table.

COMPARISONS

Many adjectives have three degrees: positive, comparative, and superlative.

✓ happy (positive), happier (comparative), happiest (superlative)

Longer adjectives form their comparative and superlative forms with the words *more* and *most*.

✓ curious, more curious, most curious

When comparing two (and only two) things, use a comparative adjective.

✓ Of the two stars, Tara is the stupider.

When comparing more than two things, use a superlative adjective.

✓ Nick is the most attractive man in all of L.A.

Some adjectives do not have comparative degrees. For example, no one can be *more pregnant* than another person. And some words like *best* and *worst* are already superlative forms. Such absolute adjectives have no comparative or superlative forms, although they may pop up in casual expressive writing and dialogue.

UNGRAMMATICAL: Chief Taft took one look and said, "He's deader than dead."

✓ Chief Taft took one look and said, "He's dead."

UNGRAMMATICAL: Sean squealed, "This is the bestest birthday I've ever had."

✓ Sean squealed, "This is the best birthday I've ever had!"

MULTIPLE ADJECTIVES

Repeated adjectives should be separated by a comma or dashes.

✓ I am very, very happy.

✓ Every, *every* teenager has seen this movie.

If you want to describe a noun with two or more adjectives in a row, separate those adjectives with commas.

✓ Trent's soothing, melodious voice captivated Rose.

Note that some adjective-noun pairs are treated as one item. In cases like these, don't separate the adjective(s) and the noun with a comma.

✓ Sylvia stared longingly at the little red Corvette.

Here, the adjective *little* describes the adjective-noun pair *red Corvette*.

PROPER ADJECTIVES

Proper adjectives, which come from proper names, should be capitalized.

✓ She brought back a lovely Vietnamese wall hanging.

✓ Iago is my favorite Shakespearean character.

Some proper adjectives have lost their associations with the names from which they were originally derived and should not be capitalized. Check with a dictionary.

✓ I love greasy french fries.

ADVERBS

Adverbs describe or modify verbs, adjectives, or other adverbs.

✓ smoothly, very, often, hopefully

Many adverbs have three degrees: positive, comparative, and superlative.

✓ little (positive), less (comparative), least (superlative)

✓ beautifully (positive), more beautifully (comparative), most beautifully (superlative)

COMPARISONS

When comparing two (and only two) things, use a comparative adverb.

✓ Sheldon sings more beautifully than his brother does.

When comparing three or more things, use a superlative adverb.

✓ Of all the kids in fourth grade, Sheldon's brother lies the most smoothly.

Some adverbs don't have comparative or superlative degrees. These include time-related adverbs like *immediately*, *now*, *last*, *first*, and so on.

INCORRECT: Firstliest, Quentin read aloud from his journal.

✓ First, Quentin read aloud from his journal.

Use adverbs only in moderation, particularly when you're writing dialogue. It's much better to use *said* over and over than to fill your dialogue with words like *despairingly*, *encouragingly*, *huffily*, and so on. Try to convey the mood you're after without relying on adverbs. Instead of writing, *"To hell with you!" Ursula cried furiously*, try something like *"To hell with you!" Ursula cried, throwing her plate across the room.*

PLACEMENT IN SENTENCE

Be sure to put an adverb as close as possible to the word it is modifying. Otherwise, confusion may result.

UNCLEAR: Gabrielle likes to show off secretly.

It's not clear whether Gabrielle likes to show off in secret or whether she secretly likes the opportunity to show off.

CLEAR: Gabrielle secretly likes to show off.

ALSO CLEAR: Gabrielle likes to show off in secret.

VERB PHRASES

When modifying a verb phrase like *could appreciate, will do, should land,* and so on, you can put the adverb right before the verb. Don't worry that you're creating the equivalent of a split infinitive—you're not.

✓ The Lost Boys could potentially appreciate Hook's good qualities.

✓ Wendy swears she will definitely do the dishes sometime soon.

✓ Peter should certainly land in Neverland by five o'clock tonight.

ADVERSE vs. AVERSE

adverse: opposed; bad

✓ Thalia ate Doritos every day for lunch and suffered no adverse effects.

averse: feeling unwilling; experiencing distaste

✓ Thalia's mother was averse to the idea of an all-Dorito lunch.

AFFECT vs. EFFECT

Affect and *effect* are mixed up all the time. *Affect*, used as a verb, means "to influence."

✓ Quinn's wild partying on Thursday night affected her performance on the history test.

Effect, used as a noun, means "result."

✓ Quinn's wild partying on Thursday night had a terrible effect on her performance on the history test.

Occasionally, *effect* may be used to mean "to bring about."

✓ Try as they might, the members of the student council could not effect real change to the school's lunch policy.

The verbs *effect* and *affect* are similar but not interchangeable. To *effect* is to cause; to *affect* is to influence.

> One trick that might help you remember the difference between the two: *a*, the first letter in the word *affect*, comes before *e*, the first letter of *effect*. This makes sense, because something is *affected* first, and the result is an *effect*. For example: "My brilliant application essay *affected* my chances of admission; the essay's *effect* was an acceptance letter."

AFTERWARD vs. AFTERWORD

afterward: at a later time, after something else (*adv.*)
✓ We surfed all day; afterward, we slept on the beach.

afterword: the text that follows a novel, etc.; literally, the *word after* (*n.*)
✓ Sprawled on the sand, I flipped open my novel and turned to the afterword.

AGGRAVATE vs. IRRITATE

aggravate: to worsen; to intensify
✓ Sal aggravated his poison ivy by scratching it incessantly.

irritate: to annoy
✓ Sal, irritated by his poison ivy, snapped at his girlfriend.

ALL READY vs. ALREADY

all ready: entirely prepared
✓ We are all ready to go skiing.

already: by now
✓ Kaylee has already completed her application to Harvard.

ALL TOGETHER vs. ALTOGETHER

all together: as one; united in the same place

✓ How lovely that we are all together on Thanksgiving.

altogether: entirely

✓ Priscilla is altogether fed up with her family.

ALLUDE vs. ELUDE

allude: to make reference

✓ Fearing his fiancée's wrath, Brian tried not to allude to his upcoming bachelor party.

elude: to avoid

✓ The dancer managed to elude Brian by hiding behind a cake.

ALLUSION vs. ILLUSION

allusion: reference

✓ Despite his heavy-handed allusion to cash, Sheila didn't seem to realize that Marty was trying to bribe her.

illusion: false image

✓ Sheila's seeming innocence is just an illusion; she is actually a hardheaded businesswoman.

ALTAR vs. ALTER

altar: table (*n.*)

✓ The priest laid the cloth on the altar.

alter: to change (*v.*)

✓ The tailor down the street alters Father Quinn's cassocks for free.

AND, BUT, AND BECAUSE

You've probably had a teacher or two who absolutely forbid you to start sentences with *but* or *and*. That teacher was mostly right. It's not a good idea to pepper your writing with these kinds of sentences. Still, the occasional sentence-starting *but* or *and* can be effective.

✓ Josh thought he had a great plan. But everything started to go terribly wrong when the hamburgers exploded.

In this example, the sentence-starting *but* injects a little drama into the proceedings. It suggests that whatever happened before was really bad.

✓ Ophelia sensed bad weather ahead. And sure enough, the skies opened after dinner.

Again, the sentence-starting *and* adds emphasis and drama. But if you use this trick too often, the effect is lost.

ANY ONE vs. ANYONE

any one: any single person or thing

✓ Show me any one person who likes sardines, and I'll give you ten bucks.

anyone: any person

✓ Anyone who likes sardines is crazy.

ANY WAY vs. ANYWAY

any way: in any fashion
- ✓ Any way you slice it, Nick doesn't want to eat a croque monsieur.

anyway: in any case, regardless
- ✓ Anyway, Nick doesn't want to go to Paris.

A PART vs. APART

a part: one piece (*n.*)
- ✓ A part of me thinks we should break up.

apart: not together (*adv.*)
- ✓ When we're apart, I'm ecstatic.

APOSTROPHES

USES
An apostrophe is used to show ownership or possession.
- ✓ Elaine's tomato soup; the water's source; the men's outrage

An apostrophe is used to signal letter omission in contractions.
- ✓ Don't tell me that I'm beautiful; it's obvious enough.

Some people like to use an apostrophe plus *s* to make certain words and terms plural; others prefer to skip the apostrophe and just use *s*. For example, the *New York Times* writes *CD's* when they're talking about more than one CD; other newspapers just say *CDs*.

Both ways are correct; inclusion of the apostrophe is a matter of preference. Whichever way you choose, be sure to stay consistent.
- ✓ Todd introduced DJ Red on the ones and twos.

Add an apostrophe plus *s* to phrases to make them plural.

✓ I can't bear to hear any more "without a doubt's" from you!

POSSESSIVES

For most words, simply add an apostrophe and *s*.

✓ The men's locker room is dirtier than the women's.

Add an apostrophe plus *s* to the end of singular words that end in *s*.

✓ Yolanda read Charles Dickens's *A Christmas Carol*.

✓ Massachusetts's baseball team infuriated Boston fans for years.

✓ The boss's tone seemed off.

The exception is words that end in an *eez* sound. Add an apostrophe only.

✓ Sophocles' sandals gave him blisters.

Note that it is not incorrect to add just an apostrophe to all words that end in *s*.

ALSO OK: Yolanda read Charles Dickens' *A Christmas Carol*.

ALSO OK: Massachusetts' baseball team infuriated Boston fans for years.

ALSO OK: The boss' tone seemed off.

We at SparkNotes prefer to be guided by pronunciation: since we hear an *uhz* sound at the end of class in *class's disappointment*, we write the *s*.

Add an apostrophe to the end of plural words that end in *s*.

✓ We're jealous of the Joneses' new lawn mower.

✓ The stars' light illuminated the path through the woods.

If two words are a unit, you need only one apostrophe plus *s*.

✓ Peanut butter and jelly's main appeal is its combination of saltiness and sweetness.

✓ My mother and father's house smells like orchids.

Be careful, though—sometimes two words appear to be a unit but are not. In those cases, each word gets an apostrophe plus *s*.

✓ Cynthia always sends flowers on her mother's and father's birthdays.

✓ Rand's and Machievelli's philosophies inspired the cruel man.

Confused about a particularly tricky apostrophe rule? Avoid the issue altogether! Don't forget, you can always avoid a gruesome phrase like *the Andrewses' most famous song* by substituting *the most famous song of the Andrews sisters*, or something similar. In a pinch, swap *of* for the troublesome apostrophe plus *s*, and you're in the clear.

APPOSITIVES

An *appositive* phrase comes after a noun and reidentifies it.

✓ The writer Donna Tartt is short and dark-haired.

Donna Tartt is an appositive phrase that renames *the writer*.

✓ I dedicate this song to Matthew Blanchard, my brother and best friend.

My brother and best friend is an appositive phrase that renames *Matthew Blanchard*.

RESTRICTIVE APPOSITIVES

Appositives that add pertinent new information are called *restrictive*. In *The writer Donna Tartt is short and dark-haired*, the appositive phrase *Donna Tartt* is restrictive: it restricts the field of all possible writers to *the writer Donna Tartt*.

Restrictive appositives should not be set off by commas from the rest of the sentence.

✓ The vampire slayer Buffy is always well groomed.

NONRESTRICTIVE APPOSITIVES

Appositives that add no necessary new information are called *nonrestrictive*. In *I dedicate this song to Matthew Blanchard, my brother and best friend*, the information added by the appositive phrase *my brother and best friend* is not necessary to understanding the sentence; the name *Matthew Blanchard* is identification enough. The appositive phrase in this sentence is nonrestrictive.

Nonrestrictive appositives should be set off by commas from the rest of the sentence.

✓ I listen to my favorite song, "Street Spirit," at least seven times a day.

Commas or no commas? Take a look at the main subject of the sentence. Is there only one of its kind? Then you need to set off the appositive phrase with commas. Otherwise, you don't.

For example, in *My mother Ethel hoed the backyard*, the main subject is *my mother*. Is *my mother* the only one of its kind? Since, yes, the speaker most likely has only one mother, use commas: *My mother, Ethel, hoed the backyard*. The appositive phrase *Ethel* is nonrestrictive; it elaborates rather than identifying.

On the other hand, consider *My friend Ginger speaks Esperanto*. The main subject is *my friend*; since the speaker is likely to have more than one friend, no commas are necessary. The appositive phrase *Ginger* is restrictive: it helps identify the friend. Of course, if the speaker is a very lonely person, he might have to say *My only friend in the world, Ginger, speaks Esperanto*.

AS

See LIKE VS. AS.

AVERSE

See ADVERSE VS. AVERSE.

A WHILE VS. AWHILE

a while: a short time (*n.*)

✓ Our nap lasted only a while.

awhile: for a time (*adv.*)

✓ I think we should sleep awhile longer.

BAD vs. BADLY

It's incorrect to say you're feeling *badly*. This might seem a little coun-terintuitive; many people think that it sounds smarter to say *feeling badly*. But, for example, *Ro feels badly* could mean that Ro doesn't have a keen sense of touch.

✓ Penelope feels bad about running over Isaac's foot.

B.C.

The abbreviation B.C. stands for *before Christ*. It is used to mark years before 1 on our calendar.

We at SparkNotes prefer to use small capital letters and periods, but you may choose to use uppercase letters for simplicity and/or omit the periods.

✓ Plato died circa 350 B.C.

Because not all people believe that the byname Christ is appropriate for the biblical Jesus, some writers prefer to use the abbreviation B.C.E., which stands for *before common era* and comes after the designated year. It's your call.

✓ Plato died circa 350 B.C.E.

BECAUSE

See And, But, and Because.

BIBLIOGRAPHY

At the end of most academic works, you should include a bibliography—an alphabetized list of the books or articles consulted. This section may also be titled "Works Cited," especially if most of the entries are referenced in the body of your work. The entries should be listed in alphabetical order.

BOOKS

List the author's name, the title (in italics), the location of the publishing company, the publishing company, and the year of publication.

✓ Tillman, Joseph. *The Works of Weird Al.* New York: Record & Reed, 2001.

EDITORS AND TRANSLATORS

List the author's name first, followed by the title of the book (in italics), the name(s) of the editor(s) and/or translator(s), the location of the publishing company, the publishing company, and the year of publication.

✓ Erdem, Erhan. *Oh, Champs-Elysees!* Edited by Renee Duchamps. Translated by Suzanna Carr. Paris: EMA, 1997.

TWO AUTHORS

List the authors in the order in which they're listed on the title page, the title of the book (in italics), the location of the publishing company, the publishing company, and the year of publication. Only the first author's name need be last name first.

✓ Isaacson, Anna, and Keeshon Smith. *The Brooklyn Cyclones: A Tale of Minor League Magic.* London: St. James Press, 2005.

REPEATED AUTHOR

To cite two or more books by the same author, list the information in full the first time around, as described above. In the following entry or entries, replace the author's name with three dashes.

✓ Medvedovsky, Betsy. *Berlin Is for Lovers.* Boston: Flamingo Books, 2005.

———. *Found in Translation: Tales from a Language Lab.* New York: SparkNotes, 2005.

ARTICLES

List the author's name, the title of the article (in quotation marks), the name of the periodical in which the article appeared (in italics), the volume number of the periodical, the date the article appeared, and the pages on which the article appeared.

✓ Barnett, Laurie. "The Truth About Dogs." *Pet Fancy* 4 (2003): 2–6.

BORN VS. BORNE

Both words are past participles of *to bear*.

born: used to describe babies

✓ Keisha was born on December 25, 2001.

borne: used in all other contexts

✓ Keisha's mother has borne two children.

✓ Borne away by a gust of wind last week, Keisha's nappy finally floated to the ground this morning.

BRACKETS

Brackets are used in quotations to mark added or altered material.

✓ According to the expert, "CFCs [chlorofluorocarbons] are a damaging pollutant."

The writer explains what CFCs are in brackets.

✓ "'I'm Henri's sister,' said [Claudette]."

The writer changes the exact quotation—"'I'm Henri's sister,' said she"—for clarity.

Try to alter quoted material as little as possible. Use brackets to replace words only when absolutely necessary.

CAPITALIZATION CHANGES

In very formal writing, brackets are used to show that capitalization has been changed. In most writing, it's okay to simply change capital letters at the beginning of quotations to lowercase. For more on this, see QUOTATIONS.

✓ When the raft sank beneath the waves, "[t]he people on shore gasped."

PUNCTUATION

Put punctuation marks outside of brackets, not inside them.

✓ "Scared by the dog, Brett called out to his mother [Judy Quinn]."

✓ "[Austen], for fear of seeming unladylike, hid her writing whenever anyone entered the room."

✓ "Imogen thinks the best park in the world is New York's [Central Park]; she visits it almost every week."

✓ "'Why do you say [you hate me]?' asked Tim."

BRAND NAMES

You're under no legal obligation to use the © symbol, or the ® symbol, or even the ™ symbol in your writing—and you probably shouldn't use these symbols, since they clutter up the page.

BRAND NAMES

Capitalize brand names.

✓ Pepsi, Sony, the Gap

There are a few classically tricky brand names that many people assume are generic.

✓ Kleenex, Xerox, Ping-Pong, Band-Aid, Laundromat

These words are losing their trademark status and are sometimes written in lowercase.

COMPUTER TERMS

Proper names should be capitalized.

✓ Microsoft, Windows XP, AOL, Internet Explorer

BRING vs. TAKE

bring: to bear here

✓ I bring home the trashy magazines from the dentist's office.

take: to bear there

✓ I take my toothbrush to the sink.

BRITICISMS

British English and American English are quite different. Try to avoid Briticisms in your writing. Here are just a few of the many variant spellings:

BRITISH	AMERICAN
afterwards	afterward
backwards	backward
burnt	burned
colour	color
downwards	downward
forwards	forward
grey	gray
Mr, Mrs, Dr	Mr., Mrs., Dr.
theatre	theater
towards	toward
upwards	upward

Their billionaires are richer and their pints are bigger: believe it or not, the British use *billion* to mean *one million million*, not *one thousand million*, as the Yanks use it. To add insult to injury, their pints are four ounces bigger than ours.

BUT

See AND, BUT, AND BECAUSE.

CAPITALIZATION

AFTER COLONS
To capitalize or not to capitalize after colons? Opinion varies. Spark-Notes almost always keeps words after colons lowercased. Even if a colon precedes a complete sentence, we don't capitalize the word after the colon.

✓ After work, Theodora picked up three items at the store: lotion, bobby pins, and a fashion magazine.

✓ Nigel and Emmanuelle hatched a brilliant plan: they would forge a note and go to the lake for the day.

Note that proper names following colons should always be capitalized.

✓ Mr. Roberts's class is full of superstars: Mandy, for example, is a baton twirler of the highest caliber.

Colons may be used to introduce lines of dialogue, as in a play script. Follow normal capitalization rules.

✓ JACK: Come on, just calm down.
   BELINDA: Don't you dare patronize me!

ETHNIC GROUPS
Capitalize the names of ethnic groups.

✓ Nearly every group on campus was represented, including Caucasians, African Americans, Arabs, Latinos, and Asians.

FOR EMPHASIS
It's usually a bad idea to capitalize entire words for emphasis. Don't use full caps unless you have a truly compelling reason for doing the written equivalent of screaming.

UNDESIRABLE: Nicky considered the painting UNBELIEVABLY beautiful.

BETTER: Nicky considered the painting unbelievably beautiful.

GRADES

Capitalize grades.

✓ As punishment for the two Fs on his report card, Oscar was grounded for a week.

PLACE NAMES

In general, don't capitalize words that come from place names.

✓ french fries, roman numeral, swiss cheese

PLACES

Don't capitalize words that suggest general location.

✓ A north wind brought snow, delighting the students.

✓ Sharrod's southern accent charmed the ladies.

Capitalize words that stand in for proper names of locations.

✓ A typical easterner, Kate felt out of place in the South.

Capitalize nicknames for places.

✓ Before he turned forty, Gus had lived in the Big Apple, Silicon Valley, the Sunshine State, and the Lone Star State.

Capitalize words like *street*, *boulevard*, and *lane* only if they follow street names.

✓ Take a right on Orchard Street. The next street on the left is ours.

Capitalize the names of buildings.

✓ Mrs. Hannigan wanted the place to shine like the top of the Chrysler Building.

Capitalize words like *federation*, *empire*, *state*, and *kingdom* only if they are part of a place name.

✓ During his visit to the United Kingdom, Howard ate hundreds of pub lunches.

QUESTIONS IN SENTENCES

If a question is asked within a sentence, the first word of that question need not begin with a capital letter.

✓ The question becomes, why do I crave french fries so desperately?

✓ Ms. Astrid's languid query, is that all there is? worried her audience.

QUOTATIONS

When quoting text, heed basic grammar rules. If the text you want to quote begins with a capital letter, but the construction of your sentence demands a lowercase letter, you may use brackets to indicate that you've changed the text.

✓ According to Alcott, "[l]ove is a great beautifier."

When omitting text from a quotation, capitalize the first word after an ellipsis (. . .) if that word is the beginning of a full sentence.

✓ "The most winning woman I ever knew was hanged for poisoning three little children. . . . [T]he most repellent man of my acquaintance is a philanthropist who has spent nearly a quarter of a million upon the London poor."

RELIGIOUS WORDS

The question of whether or not to capitalize religious words is an individual one. SparkNotes capitalizes *God* but does not capitalize *he* or *his* in relation to God.

✓ In Sunday school, the kids study God and His word.
✓ In Sunday school, the kids study God and his word.

TITLES OF WORKS

Capitalize the major words in a title.

✓ We recently saw *How to Succeed in Business Without Really Trying*.

Don't capitalize minor short words—articles (*a, an, the*), coordinating conjunctions (*and, but, nor, or, yet*), and short prepositions (*to, on, in,* etc.).

✓ We recently saw *A Funny Thing Happened on the Way to the Forum*.

How short is short? It's a matter of personal preference; we recommend capitalizing five-letter and longer prepositions.

✓ I've never read *Travels with Charlie* nor heard "Over the River and Through the Woods."

We also recommend capitalizing all verbs and pronouns, even if they are very short.

✓ "This Is His Face: Identifying Features of Prepubescent Males"

Capitalize prepositions used adverbially, such as *on* in the phrase *you turn me on*.

✓ *Turn Up the Volume: The History of Critical Reception in Rock 'n' Roll*
✓ "Looking Out for Number One"
✓ *Eight Votes For, Four Against: The Prosecution Rests*

Always capitalize the first and last words in a title.

✓ Willa listened to "Bring It On" on the way to the gym.

Capitalize the first word of a subtitle.

✓ Isaac's class studied *Patricia: The Dark Mistress of Twilight*.

PERSONAL TITLES

There is no need to capitalize titles that stand on their own. Unless titles precede names, keep them lowercased.

✓ After she was elected president of the student council, Lila insisted that everyone call her President Lila Jones.

✓ After the war, the general pontificated from his armchair.

✓ Barnard College attracts everyone from hippies to future politicians; all of its students love the college.

✓ The dean of the University cracked down on after-hours parties.

CAPITAL vs. CAPITOL

capital: a city of government

✓ As the bus approached the capital, the students cheered.

capitol: a building of government

✓ By the time they reached the capitol building, they were ready to go home.

CARDINAL NUMBERS

See NUMBERS.

CENSOR vs. CENSURE

censor: to delete offensive content

✓ Nearly all of the dirtiest jokes were censored.

censure: to criticize

✓ Viewers wrote angry letters censuring the star's rampant use of profanity.

CIRCA, CA., C.

The Latin-derived word *circa* is used with approximate dates to mean "in about." Formerly, it was conventional to italicize it in text, but these days italics are not necessary.

✓ *Beowulf* was written circa A.D. 1000.

It is frequently used in its abbreviated forms, *c.* or *ca.*, especially in scholarly texts.

✓ The works of William Shakespeare (c. 1564–1616) plague many a confused high-school student.

✓ Susie Q. lost her virginity ca. 1985, in a sunny college dorm.

CITATIONS IN TEXT

SPARKNOTES ULTIMATE STYLE

If you're including only a few quotations in your text, it's easiest to cite your sources right in the text, rather than using footnotes.

Most in-text citations will follow the quoted material. If you're citing a source for the first time in your text, list the author's name, the title (in italics), the location of the publishing company, the year of publication, and the page number. Note that the punctuation separating these items differs from the punctuation separating items in bibliography citations. Note also that closing punctuation goes outside, not inside, the parentheses.

✓ When she hears a hiss, Vera thinks of "escaped pet boa constrictors, alligators in the sewers, all manner of deceptively domesticated animals" (Francine Prose, *Bigfoot Dreams* [New York: Henry Holt, 1986], 157).

If a quotation ends with a question mark or an exclamation point, and the quotation is placed at the end of a sentence, keep the original mark and place a period after the closing parentheses.

✓ Hermione asks, "'But leaving me apart, Rupert; do you think the children are better, richer, happier, for all this knowledge; do you really think they are?" (D. H. Lawrence, *Women in Love*, 55).

The second time you cite a source, and thereafter, you don't need to include all the information about the source.

✓ Vera "can't imagine an answer that doesn't make the hippo kid in his hippo T-shirt seem like somebody's mean joke" (Prose, *Bigfoot Dreams*, 57).

If you're citing just one source in your work, you can shorten the citations even more. List the information in full once, and then simply reference page numbers or, in the case of plays, act, scene, and line numbers.

✓ In a "fiery" mood, Ivanhoe "lent but a deaf ear to the prior's grave advices and facetious jests" (453).

MID-SENTENCE QUOTATIONS

Quotations placed in mid-sentence should be cited at the end of the sentence. You don't need to cite the work directly after the closing quotation mark.

✓ In contrast to Nick Carraway's house, which is "an eyesore," Gatsby's residence is an immense mansion modeled after a French hotel (Fitzgerald, *The Great Gatsby*, 9).

CITATION PRECEDING QUOTATION

Occasionally, you'll find that a citation fits better before a quotation, rather than after it. In this case, you don't need to include every last detail about the source.

✓ In the first chapter of J. R. R. Tolkien's *The Hobbit* (Ballantine Books, 1965), hobbits are described as "a little people, about half our height, and smaller than the bearded Dwarves."

CITE, SIGHT, AND SITE

cite: to refer to (v.)

✓ James planned to cite the example of Conan O'Brien in his commencement address.

sight: something to see, vision (n.); to see (v.)

✓ At the sight of James in his cap and gown, Mrs. Chiarelli burst into tears.

site: place (n.)

✓ On this site, Conan O'Brien addressed a Harvard class.

CLAIMS, INFLATED

In your writing, try to avoid all inflated and unprovable claims. Your readers will trust you more if you avoid saying things like *Emily Dickinson clearly hated her father*, or *James Joyce is the most talented writer of all time*, or *Nothing is more painful than childbirth*. Stick to the facts, Jack.

CLICHÉS

It's easy to fill your writing with clichés. They're probably the first thing you think of when you're groping for a metaphor (*quick as . . . a wink!*) or trying to express a common emotion (*she decided there must be other fish in the sea*). Clichés might spring unbidden into your mind as you're happily typing away.

But resist all temptation! If you use clichés, your readers will be bored instantly. They will stop paying attention at least for the duration of the cliché, and probably for several phrases or sentences after that. Why say *the tearstained letter* when you could say *the letter, salted with furious tears*? Why say *vanished without a trace* when you could say *crept away, unnoticed and unmourned*?

Rid your writing of all those sayings, metaphors, and turns of phrase you've heard on countless sitcoms and read in bad novels. Force yourself to be original.

COLLOQUIAL EXPRESSIONS

Approach colloquial expressions with caution. It's fine to say *whaddup* in an email but definitely not fine to say *whaddup* or even *what's up* in an academic paper. Also, note that profanities should be avoided in formal writing, as should slang.

The inclusion of the occasional bit of slang works well in some articles and papers, but exercise caution. High school teachers are not likely to approve of slang-addled papers, and colloquialisms would be out of place in certain articles or papers. It's safest to avoid the issue altogether by writing bright, colorful, but formal prose.

COLONS

USES

Colons elaborate on what comes before them.

- ✓ Anthony's logic is sound: without pancakes, he says, syrup is useless.
- ✓ Carl was a talented guy: his many skills included playing bass guitar, drawing hilarious cartoons, and talking politics.

Colons introduce lists.

- ✓ The costume contest winners exhibited three qualities: imaginativeness, ingenuity, and sewing prowess.

Be careful: colons shouldn't introduce lists that are already introduced by verbs or prepositions.

- ✓ Margaret's thrilling summer work options include mowing lawns, serving hamburgers, and babysitting.
- ✓ Manny can't wait to don his Red Sox cap, go to Yankee Stadium, and pick a fight.

Colons signal definitions.

- ✓ *Hipster*: a bespectacled, trucker-hat-wearing inhabitant of Williamsburg

Colons can introduce commands.

- ✓ You, in the blue fedora: tell me where we can find some prairie dogs.

CAPITALIZATION

In almost all cases, keep words after colons lowercased. Even if a colon precedes a complete sentence, don't capitalize the word after the colon.

- ✓ Listen to me: we must leave on the boat right away.

Capitalize only if two or more complete sentences follow colons.

- ✓ Petra debated with herself: She could tell Tim about the toilet paper stuck to his shoe. On the other hand, she could keep quiet and let him look like an idiot.

Capitalize after colons if you're writing dialogue.

✓ MARIA: Where do you get the nerve?
  RICHARD: Maria, I prefer to call it bravery.

Note that proper names following colons should always be capitalized.

✓ The excuses were especially creative today: Hunter, for example, claimed a secret interview with the C.I.A. had prevented him from finishing his homework.

When it comes to capitalizing subtitles that follow colons, the rule is easy to remember: always capitalize them.

✓ Brenda's favorite book is *Weird Al: The Singer Speaks*.

✓ *Spot: A Dog's Life* is told from a puppy's perspective.

COMMAS

Commas, those little curly marks, separate ideas in sentences. They're required in some cases and optional in others.

ADJECTIVES
If you have a few adjectives in a row, you should separate them with commas.

✓ Annie longed for flowing, curly, golden locks.

If adjectives and the noun they describe add up to one basic idea, you don't need a comma.

✓ Annie hated her boring brown hair.

DATES
If you're naming the month, the day, and the year, insert commas around the year.

✓ Angelo's parents married on June 1, 1952, in a small chapel in Mexico.

DESCRIPTIVE PHRASES
If you've named a noun and want to describe it further, surround that further description with commas.

✓ Ms. Snidely, the hall monitor, chased Sarah through the school.

✓ Sarah, keen on evading fast-running Ms. Snidely, dashed into the broom closet.

ETC.

If you use *etc.*, or other phrases like it (*and so on, and so forth*), surround it with commas.

✓ The speaker blathered on about love, heartbreak, loss, etc., until most of the audience was fast asleep.

FOR EXAMPLE

If you're using the phrase *for example* (or similar phrases like *that is, namely*, and so on), you should insert a comma hard on its heels.

✓ Wedding cakes can be outrageously expensive; Helena, for example, spent over one thousand dollars on hers.

INTRODUCTORY PHRASES

Place commas after introductory phrases.

✓ Disgusted with her brother, Tina ran off to tattle.
✓ With a shimmy of his hips, Pete kicked off the talent show.
✓ After cheerleading practice, Darlene curled up with *War and Peace*.
✓ Without further ado, Opie presented the speaker.

Some introductory words or phrases are so brief that they don't really require a comma. In these cases, comma use is a matter of personal preference.

OK: Yesterday evening Steve took Allie to the drive-in.

ALSO OK: Yesterday evening, Steve took Allie to the drive-in.

INTRODUCTORY WORDS

Do not use commas after coordinating conjunctions (*but, so, and, yet*, and so on).

✓ So you might want to check that out.
✓ And every secretary from Jude to Ally has been insufferably rude.

LISTS

Separate items in a list with commas.

✓ Please get out your passports, boarding passes, and photo I.D.'s.

If conjunctions separate the items in a list, no commas are necessary.

✓ Do you have your passport and your boarding pass and your photo I.D.?

NAMES

When addressing someone, set off his or her name with commas.

✓ Cat, you're getting hysterical.

✓ Please, sir, step aside.

✓ Please take your seats, class.

✓ Mr. Panday, thank you for lunch.

NOT ONLY

Phrases beginning with *not only* can be set off or not set off with commas. In some instances commas provide a necessary pause, and in other instances they're merely clutter. Let your ear guide you.

UNDESIRABLE: We devoured, not only a large pizza, but also an entire carton of fried chicken.

BETTER: We devoured not only a large pizza but also an entire carton of fried chicken.

UNDESIRABLE: We drove to the hospital not only suffering from severe stomach pains but also full of remorse.

BETTER: We drove to the hospital, not only suffering from severe stomach pains, but also full of remorse.

OMITTED WORDS

One of the more magical qualities of commas is their ability to replace omitted words.

✓ Roger prefers Paris; Theodora, Rome; Vince, San Juan.

PARENTHETICAL INFORMATION

Set off nonessential words or phrases with commas.

✓ The trip was, shall we say, eventful.

✓ When it comes to Ohio, however, emotions run high.

✓ Mina, as she enjoyed her massage, decided to have salmon for lunch.

✓ The play, while far from terrible, was not ready for Broadway.

QUOTATIONS

Introduce quotations with commas.

✓ She cried, "You know I loathe dogs!"

SERIAL COMMAS

Everyone agrees that items in a series should be separated with commas. But not everyone agrees that the serial comma, which comes before the conjunction in a list, is necessary.

NO SERIAL COMMA: Today we learned about bug bites, poison ivy and rashes.

SERIAL COMMA: Today we learned about bug bites, poison ivy, and rashes.

SparkNotes is strongly in favor of the serial comma. We think it makes prose clearer and more readable—which is, after all, the point of punctuation.

TWO CONJUNCTIONS

If two conjunctions (like *but* and *if*) appear next to each other, you don't need to separate them with a comma.

UNDESIRABLE: I'm no expert, but, if I may make a suggestion, you might want to step away from the crocodile pit.

BETTER: I'm no expert, but if I may make a suggestion, you might want to step away from the crocodile pit.

TWO SENTENCES

To join two sentences, use a comma and a conjunction.

✓ Charlie wanted to start a family, but Emily didn't like the idea.

✓ Charlie proposed, and Emily said she'd think about it.

✓ Do you want to marry me, or are you just scared to lose me?

Sometimes, the two sentences you want to join are so short that a conjunction will do the job, and you don't need a comma.

✓ Ryan looks sick and Beatrice looks sicker.

YES AND NO

When they begin sentences, *yes* and *no*, and words like them, should be followed by commas.

✓ Yes, we have no bananas.

✓ No, we're not sure that's relevant.

✓ Um, I don't think so.

✓ Well, that's your opinion.

✓ Sure, we could stay in Bali.

NO COMMAS NECESSARY

You don't need a comma between the two parts of a compound predicate.

✓ They will explain the pool rules and show you around the clubhouse.

If you're unsure about whether you need a comma, check to see if the subject changes over the course of the sentence. If it does, you need a comma.

✓ The parrot squawks obscenities, and the dog eats nothing but steak.

If the subject doesn't change, you don't need a comma.

✓ The parrot squawks obscenities and spits out its crackers.

If the last item in a list is a single unit connected by the word *and*, keep that unit comma-free.

✓ For lunch, Jenny ate carrots, applesauce, and peanut butter and jelly.

✓ Bill shouted, Bob wept, and Biff threw up his hands and stormed out.

Not all introductory phrases require commas. If the introductory phrase is directly followed by the verb it modifies, leave out the comma.

✓ Frowning down at us was the hated headmaster.

✓ Down the alley dashed Yael.

If information is crucial to the meaning of a sentence, don't set it off with commas.

✓ The restaurant with the red door is where we're meeting.

If a quotation is preceded by a word like *that*, no comma is needed.

✓ Caleb said that "there are other fish in the sea" was his least favorite saying.

COMPLEMENT vs. COMPLIMENT

complement: a worthy addition (*n.*)

✓ Violet's pink cheeks were the perfect complement to her dark eyes.

compliment: to praise (*v.*); a piece of praise (*n.*)

✓ Violet accepted the compliment with a shy blush.

COMPOUND WORDS

COMPOUND ADVERBS

Avoid compound adverbs like *heretofore*, *therefore*, and so on; they will make your writing sound brittle and overly formal.

DESCRIBING NOUNS

Hyphens, although they look tiny and insignificant, have great powers of clarification.

Use them in compound modifiers that come before nouns.

UNCLEAR: Elana's what the hell attitude always got her in trouble.

BETTER: Elana's what-the-hell attitude always got her in trouble.

Use them when a few phrases modify one noun.

UNCLEAR: That typical twenty first century guilt free attitude disgusts Moira.

CLEAR: That typical twenty-first-century guilt-free attitude disgusts Moira.

> You never need to hyphenate adverbs ending in *-ly*. For example: *a slow-burning temper*, but *a slowly burning temper*; *the fever-induced dream*, but *the feverishly dreaming boy*.

Note that it's almost always correct to hyphenate before a noun and to open up after a verb.

✓ The well-bred boy never burps after eating.

✓ Alistair, who is exceedingly well bred, pats his mouth with a napkin after every bite.

PLURALS OF COMPOUNDS

Be careful when forming the plurals of compound words. Some compound words take an *s* at the end of the last word to become plural, as do most nouns; others are trickier.

✓ attorney general ——> attorneys general

✓ court-martial ——> courts-martial

✓ mother-in-law ——> mothers-in-law

POSSESSIVE COMPOUNDS

Generally, to make compound nouns possessive, you can just add an apostrophe and an *s* to the last word.

✓ My mother-in-law's visits are always contentious.

✓ The copy chief's buffet lunch was delicious.

But in some cases, making compound nouns possessive gets hairy. If you're stumped, you might want to rework the sentence in order to avoid the problem altogether.

AWKWARD: The courts'-martial scandalous nature led to frantic press interest.

BETTER: The scandalous nature of the courts-martial led to frantic press interest.

CONDITIONAL

The conditional might trip you up or give you pause, but it's actually a wonderfully simple verb form to get right.

The formula always goes: *If . . . were . . . would*. That's it! There's nothing else to memorize.

✓ If I were principal, I would let everyone leave at eleven a.m.

Note that it's never correct to say *if . . . was . . . were*.

> The title of the song "If I Were a Rich Man" is an excellent way to remember the use of *were* with the conditional.

CONFIDANT(E) VS. CONFIDENT

confidant: someone who is trusted with secrets (*n.*)

confidante: a woman entrusted with secrets (*n.*)

✓ Nicky's confidant is the only one who knows the real story of the stolen helmet.

confident: assured (*adj.*)

✓ Nicky is confident that Becky won't reveal the sordid story of the helmet.

CONJUNCTIONS

Conjunctions are the words like *and, also, but, because, so, therefore,* and *which.* Conjunctions connect words and clauses.

ADDING INFORMATION
Additive coordinating conjunctions (*and, also, in addition,* etc.) tell you that what follows the conjunction will add information.

✓ The class jeered, and the substitute burst into tears.

BEGINNING SENTENCES WITH *AND* OR *BUT*
See AND, BUT, AND BECAUSE.

COMING TO CONCLUSIONS
Final coordinating conjunctions (*therefore, so, in consequence,* etc.) imply a course of action.

✓ The party was loud, so the neighbors called the police.

JOINING WORDS
Coordinating conjunctions simply join sentences or parts of sentences together.

✓ Diane prefers platinum, and Darla prefers gold.
✓ I'm awake but not alert.

RELATING PARTS OF A SENTENCE
Correlative conjunctions, which come in pairs (*either . . . or; neither . . . nor; not only . . . but also;* and so on), relate parts of a sentence to each other.

✓ Either Rebecca or Jason will win the Cutest Baby in South Beach contest.

When using correlative conjunctions, make sure the second conjunction is in the same part of the sentence as the first conjunction.

CONFUSING: Liam not only burned down the seats but also the stage.

✓ Liam burned down not only the seats but also the stage.
✓ Liam not only burned down the seats but also tore down the stage curtain.

SHOWING CONTRAST

Contrasting coordinating conjunctions (*nevertheless*, *but*, *although*, etc.) contrast information.

✓ The principal begged the sub to stay, but she refused violently.

SUBORDINATING INFORMATION

Subordinating conjunctions (*because*, *if*, etc.) precede clauses that are subordinate to the main clause.

✓ Brian works hard because his parents pay him for every good grade he earns.

✓ Mrs. Vespa wondered if $200 tutus were really necessary.

Participles like *assuming*, *considering*, and *provided* can function as conjunctions when they subordinate one part of a sentence to another.

✓ We'll arrive around eleven, assuming Angelina drives.

✓ This coffee is worth every penny, considering that it helps me stay awake to study.

CONTRACTIONS

A *contraction* is the combination of two words by means of an apostrophe—which usually replaces a letter or two. Common contractions include *it's* (*it* + *is*), *you're* (*you* + *are*), *don't* (*do* + *not*), *won't* (*will* + *not*), *he's* (*he* + *is*), and so on.

Contractions cause people undue grief; many strong writers occasionally mix up *their* and *they're*, *your* and *you're*, and *its* and *it's*. For help on these matters, see the individual words.

CULTURAL TERMS

ORGANIZATIONS

In general, capitalize only the names of specific cultural and political groups.

✓ Chester is a card-carrying member of the Communist Party.

✓ Chester has certain communistic impulses.

✓ On the weekends, Mandy stumps for Democrats.

✓ In our democracy, everyone is free to eat fast food.

CULTURE

Here is a brief list of some capitalized and lowercased cultural terms.

abstract impressionism	modernism
art deco	neoclassical
baroque	pop art
Beaux-Arts	postmodernism
classical	realism
deconstruction	Romanticism
existentialism	structuralism
humanism	transcendentalism
impressionism	

HISTORICAL DOCUMENTS

Capitalize the names of historical documents.

✓ the Bill of Rights; the Constitution; the Fifth Amendment

HISTORICAL PERIODS AND EVENTS

Some names of historical periods and events are capitalized. Others are not. If you're not sure, refer to a dictionary.

✓ the Victorian era; the Renaissance; the colonial age; the civil rights movement; Prohibition; D-day

RELIGIOUS GROUPS

Capitalize the names of religious groups.

✓ Christianity, Christian; Islam, Islamic; Catholicism, Catholic; Judaism, Jewish

SCHOOLS AND INSTITUTIONS

Capitalize the names of schools and institutions.

✓ The students of Columbia University often visit the Whitney Museum.

✓ Members of the Patriots got haircuts before their visit to the White House.

✓ The National Organization for Sub-Par Golfers (NOSPG) held a meeting in Miami.

DASHES

A dash is a horizontal line of a punctuation mark—like so. Dashes shouldn't be confused with HYPHENS, which are shorter and have a different function.

BASIC USE
Dashes are used to set off explanations or related thoughts.

✓ Everything—scraped knees, loud noises, nightmares—makes Eloise cry.

✓ Nate insists on his rights as a senior—the right to bully freshmen, for example.

✓ Sadie Hawkins Day, prom queens, powder puff football games—this is the kind of prefeminist silliness our school endorses.

Dashes are also used to set off quick pauses and interruptions.

✓ Maria looked stricken. "You—you can't go!" she said.
   "But what about—"
Frederick cut me off, saying, "We can't think about that now."

SPACES
Do not use spaces either before or after dashes.

✓ Billy—you know, the freckly kid—smashed a window again.

EM DASHES AND EN DASHES
The technical name for a dash is *em dash*, to distinguish it from the shorter *en dash*. (Back in the day, em dashes were as long as a capital *M* and en dashes were as long as a capital *N*.)

If you overuse the dash, you will exhaust your readers. Some writers use dashes to cram three or four ideas into one sentence (*The work of David Eggers—that most beloved writer of thirty-somethings—while highly entertaining, and certainly high-spirited—frantic, some would say— still sells remarkably well*); some writers use them to indulge their own discursive thoughts; some writers use them because they are lazy and it is easier to compose one sprawling, dash-filled, dubiously organized sentence than it is to compose three tidy, logical sentences. If you fill your writing with dashes, you force your readers to stop and start, to back up and then plunge back into the sentence.

En dashes are used to indicate a stretch of time between dates. Note that you should never match *from* with an en dash instead of *to*, or *between* with an en dash instead of *and*.

✓ Jack attended camp every summer from 1995 to 2000.

✓ At summer camp, 1995–2000, Jack learned many annoying songs.

✓ Between March and April, the rich kids went on skiing vacations.

✓ March–April is skiing season for the rich kids.

Use an en dash when referring to someone still alive, or something ongoing.

✓ Hugh Jackman (1968–)

✓ My high school career (2003–) seems interminable.

En dashes are also used to form compounds with two-word or longer expressions.

✓ a pre–Civil War plantation

It is also acceptable to use hyphens, rather than en dashes, for both date ranges and compounds.

✓ President Bill Clinton (1993-2001) plays the saxophone.

✓ We crossed the New Mexico-Arizona border on foot.

COMPUTER USE

In Microsoft Word, insert an em dash by clicking on Insert, choosing Symbol, clicking on the Special Characters tab, and then choosing Em Dash. You can also insert an em dash by pressing Ctrl + Shift + Num-.

In Microsoft Word, an en dash may be inserted by clicking on Insert, choosing Symbol, clicking on the Special Characters tab, and then choosing En Dash. You can also insert an en dash by pressing Ctrl + Num-.

DATES

ABBREVIATED YEARS

When shortening a year to its last two digits, use an apostrophe.

✓ The class of '04 loathes the class of '05.

B.C., A.D., B.C.E., C.E.

The two most common pairs of abbreviations for eras are B.C. (*before Christ*) and A.D. (*anno Domini, in the year of our lord*); and B.C.E. (*before the common era*) and C.E. (*common era*). SparkNotes puts these abbreviations in small caps and places periods between the letters.

DECADES

You may spell out decades or not, according to your preference — just be consistent in your writing.

✓ Sophie loved the acid-washed jeans of the eighties.

✓ Sophie loved the teased bangs of the 1980s.

✓ Sophie loved the jelly shoes of the 80s.

When referring to decades, use *s* alone, not an apostrophe and an *s*.

✓ Braun dreamed of being a flapper in the 1920s.

CENTURIES

Spell out centuries; do not capitalize them.

✓ To Olive's dismay, the next unit is on the eighteenth century.

COMMAS

If you're naming a month, day, and year, in that order, include commas after the day and the year.

✓ On March 1, 2001, Joe was forced to shave his head after losing a bet.

If you're being pretentious and naming a day, month, and year, in that order, no commas are necessary.

✓ It was the lecture of 27 January 1999 that really drove Mr. Williams's class over the edge.

If you're naming a month and a year, no commas are necessary.

✓ In June 1950 they embarked on an exploration of the backyard.

DAYS, MONTHS, SEASONS, HOLIDAYS

Capitalize days of the week, months, and holidays. Do not capitalize seasons.

✓ My favorite winter holiday, Christmas, falls on the fourth Wednesday of December this year.

SLASHES

Don't use slashes when noting dates in formal writing.

✓ On February 14, 2005, Mark brutally rejected Tiana's valentine.

STAND-ALONE DATES

If you're mentioning a date without attaching it to a month, spell it out.

✓ Bea circled the sixteenth in red ink.

DEDUCE vs. INDUCE

deduce: to figure out; to draw a definitive conclusion

✓ Holmes deduced that his visitor was a bootblack in a mere thirty seconds.

induce: to stimulate; to observe and then make a decent guess

✓ Dr. Watson induced labor, and the patient gave birth to a healthy girl.

✓ After Holmes explained his thought process, Watson induced that Holmes always looks at his visitors' hands and feet.

DEFINITE vs. DEFINITIVE

definite: unambiguous

✓ Toby has a definite talent for alienating people.

definitive: authoritative

✓ The definitive guide to failing in the publishing world is called *How to Lose Friends and Alienate People*.

DEFUSE vs. DIFFUSE

defuse: to calm (*v.*)

✓ Olaf defused the tense situation with soothing words.

diffuse: scattered (*adj.*); to scatter (*v.*)

✓ The diffuse tensions at the family reunion made Olaf very anxious.

DESERT vs. DESSERT

desert: to abandon (*v.*); a hot, sandy place (*n.*)

✓ His strength had all but deserted him when he finally reached the oasis.

✓ Walter trudged through the desert, longing for a piece of chocolate cake and a glass of milk.

dessert: a sweet following a meal (*n.*)

✓ Parched and starving, Walter devoured a steak and then asked for dessert.

DIALOGUE

Dialogue, or reported speech between several people or characters, is commonly enclosed in quotation marks and set off with commas from the rest of the sentence. Most commonly, each new speaker begins a new paragraph.

✓ "I don't think I like Mrs. Schwein-Bazel," said Daisy with a heavy sigh. "Yesterday, she poked me in the shoulder with her ugly red ruler."

Ginger nodded. "Do you think," she asked in a tinny voice, "that she's a witch?"

Daisy thought carefully and then replied, "I would expect a witch to have more warts."

BEGINNING QUOTATIONS

A quotation may or may not start a sentence. Either way, a complete sentence should start with a capital letter.

✓ "Why, pray tell, did you give me a giant stuffed cactus for Christmas?" asked Julia.

✓ Her mother spat back, "Because you're as prickly as a cactus thorn."

Be sure to put the comma after a word like *said* or *replied* outside the opening quotation mark.

ENDING QUOTATIONS

If the quotation ends the sentence, then keep its original punctuation. The sentence will end with the closing quotation mark.

✓ Julia remarked, "But a stuffed cactus isn't really very prickly, is it?"

✓ Julia shouted, "You're insufferable!"

✓ Julia pulled herself together. "I am leaving."

If the quotations ends in a period, change that period to a comma if the sentence keeps going after the closing quotation mark. Do not change exciting end punctuation like question marks and exclamation points, even if the sentence keeps going.

✓ "Don't you agree, Mr. Tweely?" asked Emily with a sly smile.

✓ "Absolutely not!" he replied.

✓ "A pity," replied Emily coolly.

UNFINISHED SPEECH

Use an ellipsis to indicate that a speaker has trailed off.

✓ "I don't think . . . That is, I'd prefer to come back later."

✓ "She hesitated. "Well, if you wish . . . "

Use a dash to indicate an interruption or an abrupt stop.

✓ "Actually, my parents hate—" Sarah caught herself. "I'll tell them you stopped by."

SPELLING OUT

Spell out most words in dialogue. In particular, spell out all numbers.

✓ "I gave her seventy-five dollars to pay for the damages, but she still wouldn't return Fluffy!"

If the dialogue involves complicated numbers, it may be clearer to use numerals.

✓ "I paid him $135.26 to get his phone number: 095-386-2947."

DIFFUSE

See DEFUSE VS. DIFFUSE.

DIRECTIONS

Do not capitalize directions.

✓ Auntie Rita heads south every winter, like a migrating bird.

Do, however, capitalize the names of regions.

✓ Auntie Rita goes to the South because she loves grits.

DISCREET VS. DISCRETE

discreet: cautious

✓ With a discreet gesture, Toni indicated that J.T. had poppy seeds in his teeth.

discrete: separate

✓ Eight discrete poppy seeds were dislodged with dental floss.

DISINTERESTED VS. UNINTERESTED

disinterested: neutral, unbiased
✓ The best judges are disinterested.

uninterested: bored, not interested
✓ Uninterested in his homework, Martin nodded off.

DOUBLE NEGATIVES

Double negatives are two negative words placed next to each other. This is never correct and will often imply the opposite of what is intended.

UNDESIRABLE: When Mama ain't happy, ain't nobody happy.
BETTER: When Mama isn't happy, nobody is happy.

UNDESIRABLE: Suzanna can't scarcely wait for homecoming.
BETTER: Suzanna can scarcely wait for homecoming.

EACH OTHER VS. ONE ANOTHER

Use *each other* with two people.
✓ Tim and Tina gazed into each other's eyes.

Use *one another* with more than two people.
✓ The other people in the room looked at one another, embarrassed by Tim and Tina's smooching.

EFFECT

See AFFECT vs. EFFECT.

EITHER . . . OR, NEITHER . . . NOR

If two singular subjects are connected by *neither . . . nor* or *either . . . or,* the verb must be singular as well.

✓ Neither Spiderman nor Batman is going to the party.

✓ Either Slim or Roger has to leave town before someone gets hurt.

If one singular subject and one plural subject are connected by *neither . . . nor* or *either . . . or,* match the verb with whichever subject it's closer to.

✓ Neither Olivia nor the boys eat mushrooms.

✓ Neither the boys nor Olivia eats mushrooms.

✓ Either one rat or several mice are eating everything in the cupboard.

✓ Either several mice or one rat is eating everything in the cupboard.

E.G. vs. I.E.

e.g.: for example (*exempli gratia*)

✓ Rhonda stayed only the most expensive hotels, e.g., the Maritime, the W, and the Plaza.

i.e.: that is (*id est*)

✓ Howard was the team manager—i.e., he wasn't good enough to actually play.

ELICIT vs. ILLICIT

elicit: to draw out (*v.*)

✓ In the interview, Brady skillfully elicited the celebrity's secrets.

illicit: illegal (*adj.*)

✓ The celebrity, it turned out, had done several illicit things that day.

ELLIPSES

An ellipsis consists of three points separated by spaces. It is used to indicate omission (elision) or hesitation.

SPEECH

Use ellipses to indicate confused or worried pauses in speech.

✓ "But . . . if . . . I just don't understand!"

✓ "So you . . . you cheated on me with my best friend?"

Also use ellipses to indicate trailing off.

✓ "Oh, perhaps . . . ," Angus said, staring at the meadow.

To indicate a firm interruption in dialogue, a dash is used instead. For more on this, see DIALOGUE.

QUOTATIONS

Use ellipses to indicate omitted dialogue. For detailed instructions, see QUOTATIONS.

ELUDE

See ALLUDE vs. ELUDE.

EMIGRATE vs. IMMIGRATE

emigrate: to leave one's country

✓ Antonio's grandfather emigrated from Capri in 1901.

immigrate: to move to another country

✓ Antonio's grandfather immigrated to America in 1901.

ENDNOTES

See FOOTNOTES AND ENDNOTES.

ET AL.

The Latin term *et al.* means "and others." It is used in scholarly contexts and need not be italicized.

✓ *Of Pitchers and Belly-Itchers* (Andrew Littell et al., 2002) chronicles the trials and tribulations of four Little Leaguers afflicted with chronic chicken pox.

Et al. is an abbreviation for the masculine *et alii*, the feminine *et aliae*, or the neuter *et alia*.

ET CETERA, ETC.

The Latin term *et cetera* and its common abbreviation *etc*. means "and so forth." It is used to truncate lists of things of the same type.

✓ Rudolph invited all the usual suspects—Prancer, Dancer, Vixen, etc.

EVERY DAY vs. EVERYDAY

every day: each day (*n.*)

✓ Every day after school, Xavier eats caviar.

everyday: ordinary (*adj.*)

✓ Lara eats a more everyday snack of peanut butter and crackers.

EVERY ONE vs. EVERYONE

every one: each person (*n.*)

✓ Every one of us longs for a tropical cruise.

everyone: everybody in a group (*pronoun*)

✓ Everyone on the cruise longed for a cool breeze.

EXCEPT

See ACCEPT vs. EXCEPT.

EXCLAMATION POINTS

Exclamations points indicate strong emotion, like surprise, anger, and urgency.

WITH QUESTION MARKS

We don't recommend combining exclamation points with question marks, even if you want to indicate strong emotion. Instead, choose whichever mark is more appropriate.

EXCESSIVE: Are you kidding me?!

BETTER: Are you kidding me?

EXCESSIVE: I'm in total shock!?

BETTER: I'm in total shock!

> Exclamation points should be used sparingly—even in emails. Writing filled with exclamation points sounds either hysterical or ditzy.

WITH QUOTATIONS

If exclamation points are part of quoted material, they should be included inside the quotation marks. If they are not part of the quoted material, they should be placed outside the quotation marks.

✓ That liar Brianna just told me she "would never do that"!

✓ "I would never do that!" Brianna cried.

FANCY WORDS

Many people believe they will sound smarter if they fill their writing with big words. In fact, the best writing is clean, simple, and pared down. Professional writers do not lean on ten-dollar words; they rely on strong sentence structure, original thinking, and clarity of expression. This is not to say that you should refrain from using a fancy word if it perfectly captures your meaning. But focus first and foremost on getting your meaning across to the reader, without worrying about how clever you sound.

FARTHER vs. FURTHER

farther: used with physical distance

✓ The farther we drive, the more I long to stretch my legs.

further: used with abstract distance or depth

✓ Elvira decided to investigate the matter further.

FAZE vs. PHASE

faze: to disturb (*v.*)

✓ Gerald looked a bit fazed by the scurrying rats.

phase: a stage of development (*n.*)

✓ For most people, the fear of rats is not a phase, but a lifelong state.

FAULTY COMPARISONS

Faulty comparisons occur when two things are compared inappropriately, or in a way that could confuse readers.

UNCLEAR: Mark pines for Chris more than Kitty.

This sentence could mean either that Mark pines for Chris more than Kitty pines for Chris, or that Mark pines for Chris more than he pines for Kitty.

FIXING FAULTY COMPARISONS

Make sure you are comparing two similar things.

FAULTY: Penny's phone bill is bigger than Duncan.

In the problem sentence above, the writer means to compare Penny's phone bill to Duncan's phone bill, but she winds up comparing the phone bill to Duncan. Make sure you compare object to object.

CLEAR: Penny's phone bill is bigger than Duncan's phone bill.

UNDESIRABLE: Trina goes to the ballet less than Roger.

In the problem sentence about Trina's ballet-viewing habits, going to the ballet is compared to Roger. Make sure you compare action to action.

CLEAR: Trina goes to the ballet less often than Roger does.

FEWER

See LESS VS. FEWER.

FIGURES OF SPEECH

Readers must *work* to picture a sidewalk as hot as toaster coils, a sky like a murky sea, or a blonde with legs made of rubber. So although the occasional simile or metaphor can sparkle, especially if it is unique and likely to strike the reader as true, avoid filling your writing with figures of speech. After a while, your readers will give up or grow resentful.

FLARE VS. FLAIR

flare: a light

✓ The distant flare signaled to the ship.

flair: a talent

✓ Ahab has a real flair for chasing whales.

FOOTNOTES AND ENDNOTES

Both footnotes and endnotes are used to cite sources or make comments. Footnotes appear at the bottom of the page; endnotes appear at the end of a paper or a book, in a separate section.

WHEN TO INCLUDE NOTES

If you're working on a research paper, or any paper that draws on multiple sources, you'll want to include footnotes or endnotes. You don't need to use notes if you're referencing only, for example, the edition of Shakespeare's *Much Ado About Nothing* that everyone in class is using.

In that case, you can refer to acts, scenes, and lines within the text of the paper. (For more on in-paper references, see CITATIONS IN TEXT.)

WHAT TO FOOTNOTE

Be sure to footnote not only quoted material but also summaries of other writers' arguments. You do not need to footnote basic facts known to most experts, even if you discovered them in the work of one particular expert; you *do* need to footnote theories and points that are unique or uniquely expressed.

ARTICLES

List the author's name, the title of the article (in quotation marks), the name of the periodical in which the article appeared (in italics), the volume number of the periodical, the date on which the article appeared, and the pages in which the article appeared.

✓ Laurie Barnett, "The Truth About Dogs," *Pet Fancy* 4 (2003): 2–6.

On the second mention and thereafter, list the author's last name, the title of the article (abbreviated if long), and the page number.

✓ Barnett, "The Truth About Dogs," 7.

COMMENTARY

If you want to write your own commentary in a footnote, include it after the source information.

✓ Dane, *Girl Town*, 114. This beetle was known to stimulate the appetite.

Footnotes need not always cite a source. Occasionally they can be used for your own commentary.

✓ Readers interested in Daryl's musings in this chapter might be interested in Roald Dahl's *My Uncle Oswald*, a prescient look at the same subject.

EDITORS AND TRANSLATORS

List the author's name first, followed by the title (in italics), the name(s) of the editor(s) and/or translator(s), the location of the publishing company, the publishing company, the year of publication, and the page number.

✓ Erhan Erdem, *Oh, Champs-Elysees!*, ed. Renee Duchamp, trans. Suzanna Carr (Paris: EMA, 1997), 32.

On the second mention and thereafter, include the last names only, the title, and the page number(s). Do not include the abbreviations *ed.* or *trans.*

✓ Erdem, *Oh, Champs-Elysees!*, 45–47.

IBID.

If you footnote a source and your next footnote comes from the exact same source, there is no need to repeat all of the information. Instead, use the abbreviation *ibid.*, which is short for *ibidem* ("in the same place"). This will tell your readers that you're referencing the exact same source that you referenced in the previous footnote. If the page reference is the same as in the previous footnote, use *ibid.* by itself. If the page reference is different, include it.

✓ [1] Barnett, "The Truth About Dogs," 7.
   [2] Ibid.
   [3] Ibid., 10–11.

INSERTING FOOTNOTES AND ENDNOTES

In Microsoft Word, insert footnotes or endnotes by clicking on Insert and scrolling down to Reference, then Footnote.

LONG TITLES

Note that in all footnotes, long titles (*The Brooklyn Cyclones: A Tale of Minor League Magic*) should be written out in full (in italics) in the first note. In subsequent notes, shorten the title and omit the article if it comes at the beginning of the title (*Brooklyn Cyclones*).

Do not use footnotes as a forum to express long anecdotes or as a place to squeeze in interesting effluvia from your research. Readers will flinch if they are faced with a barrage of footnotes in ten-point font that threaten to overwhelm the actual text of the paper. If the information you're tempted to turn into a footnote is important, include it in the text of the paper. If it's not essential, cut it.

ONE AUTHOR

The first time you footnote a work, list the author's name (first name first), the title (in italics), the location of the publishing company, the publishing company, the year of publication, and the page number(s).

✓ Joseph Tillman, *The Works of Weird Al* (New York: Record & Reed, 2001), 89–90.

There is no need to footnote works in full after the first time they are mentioned. After citing a book once, simply footnote the author's last name, the title (in italics), and the page number.

✓ Tillman, *The Works of Weird Al*, 114.

TWO OR MORE AUTHORS

List the authors in the order in which they're listed on the title page (first names first), the title (in italics), the location of the publishing company, the publishing company, the year of publication, and the page number(s).

✓ Anna Isaacson and Keeshon Smith, *The Brooklyn Cyclones: A Tale of Minor League Magic* (London: St. James Press, 2005), 103.

On the second mention and thereafter, include the authors' last names only, the title (in italics), and the page number(s).

✓ Isaacson and Smith, *Brooklyn Cyclones,* 110–11.

NUMBERING

In a book with chapters, the footnotes should not be numbered continuously throughout the book. Instead, the footnotes in each chapter should begin with the number 1.

Place the footnote number at the end of the sentence rather than directly after the quotation. Be sure to use superscript (text above the normal text), not normal numerals. In Microsoft Word, this can be accomplished simply by clicking Insert and choosing Reference, then Footnote.

✓ Rowlandson writes, "When they had done that, they made a fire and put them both in it"—a remark that is, typically, both restrained and dramatic.[1]

SYMBOLS

If a paper or book contains only a few quotations, you can indicate footnotes with * or † or other symbols instead of numbering the footnotes. If you choose this option, use the symbols in this order: * † ‡ §

FORMER VS. LATTER

former: the first of a pair

✓ When offered chocolate or strawberry, Charles, who hates pink, chose the former.

latter: the last of a pair

✓ When offered chocolate or strawberry, Sly, who hates brown, chose the latter.

FRAGMENTS

A sentence fragment is a phrase or clause that doesn't have a subject and a verb that make a complete sentence.

FRAGMENT: Although there is a chance of thunderstorms.

FIXING FRAGMENTS

Be particularly wary when beginning a sentence with words like *between*, *before*, *although*, and *while*. Sentences that begin with these words have a way of turning into fragments.

FRAGMENT: Between the sheets, the crumbs that made sleeping uncomfortable.

✓ Between the sheets nestled the crumbs that made sleeping uncomfortable.

> Fragments may sound correct to your ear. For one thing, they're very common in advertising. Take the following ad:
>
> *JP Morgan investment expertise. Now within your reach.*
>
> That may not strike you as grammatically objectionable, but it's actually two fragments. Corrected, the ad might read *JP Morgan investment expertise is now within your reach.*

FURTHER

See FARTHER VS. FURTHER.

GENDERED LANGUAGE

Try to avoid using *he, his,* or *him* whenever you're describing an unknown or imagined person. The constant use of male pronouns is sexist.

UNDESIRABLE: When a doctor operates, he should listen to classical music.

There are several ways to avoid reflexively referring to men. Each option has its own problems and benefits. Whichever option you choose, be sure that it is consistent in context.

ALTERNATION

You can alternate between using male and female pronouns. This option requires careful attention but also allows you to avoid some ambiguity.

✓ The student forced to rise at six o'clock won't be able to focus on his schoolwork. The student who wakes up at ten o'clock will be alert and ready to face her work. She will be less tired than he.

REWRITING

You can avoid the problem by rewriting.

✓ Students forced to rise at six A.M. won't be able to focus on their schoolwork. Students who wake up at ten A.M. will be alert and ready to face their work.

✓ The unknown culprit will face the vice principal's wrath.

S/HE AND SIMILAR

You can concoct a combination of male and female pronouns such as *she/he, s/he, him/her, his/hers.* This option can be unsightly.

✓ The culprit, whoever s/he is, will face the vice principal's wrath.

THEIR

What you *cannot* do is match a singular noun with the plural possessive *their* in an attempt to be gender neutral.

UNDESIRABLE: Someone left their prom tickets on the bench.

✓ Someone left her prom tickets on the bench.

✓ Someone left his or her prom tickets on the bench.

UNDESIRABLE: Whoever wants to go to the water park should bring their bathing suit.

✓ Whoever wants to go to the water park should bring his bathing suit.

✓ If you want to go to the water park, bring your bathing suit.

GERUNDS

See *–ING* WORDS.

GOOD VS. WELL

Good is an adjective (a word that describes nouns). *Well* is usually an adverb (a word used to describe verbs).

✓ Neil, who is notorious for his good behavior, has never shoplifted.

✓ Brian hides his anger very well.

People often use *good* when they should use *well*, especially in speech. Remember, do not use *good* to describe verbs.

✓ Shandron did well on that pop quiz.

Note that you can use *well* as an adjective when you're describing how healthy someone feels or looks.

✓ Despite her pasty appearance, Thea insisted that she felt well.

HISTORICAL TERMS

Most names of historical periods should not be capitalized.

✓ early antiquity; modern history; the colonial period

Do, however, capitalize proper names.

✓ the Victorian era; Roman history; the Civil War era

Here is a partial list of capitalized and lowercased names of historical events, groups, and periods:

CAPITALIZED

the Arab League
the Boston Tea Party
Communist
Democrat (member of the party)
the Democratic Party
the Depression
the European Union (the EU)
Fascist
the GOP
the Great Depression
the Green Party
the Industrial Revolution
the Left
NAFTA (North American Free Trade Association)
NATO (North Atlantic Treaty Organization)

Nazi
Nazism
the New Deal
Progressive movement
the Progressive Party
Prohibition
Reconstruction
Republican (member of the party)
the Republican Party
the Right
Socialist (member of the party)
the Socialist Party

LOWERCASED

anarchist
bolshevism
the civil rights movement
the cold war
communism
democracy
democratic

fascism
independent
left wing
moderate
progressive
right wing

CENTURIES AND MILLENNIA

Spell out centuries and millennia; do not capitalize them.

✓ the fifth millennium; the eighteenth century

DECADES

Decades are usually written using numbers. If the context is unclear, you might want to spell out the decade in full.

✓ the 20s; the 1990s

✓ the twenties; the nineteen-nineties

HYPHENS

You can open up compound words (*coffee mug*), hyphenate them (*donut-hole-eating*), or close them up (*coffeepot*).

> Although there are some strict rules governing when to open, when to hyphenate, and when to close, in many cases there is room for debate. Moreover, the rules that do exist are changing all the time. Often, words that are hyphenated or opened up will, over time, become closed up and accepted as one word (*e-mail* becomes *email*, for instance). Feelings on these compound matters run high, so be ready to defend the positions you choose.

DESCRIBING NOUNS

Hyphens, which look like miniature dashes, have great powers of clarification.

UNCLEAR: Pete plans to attend the oversize truck convention.

Is the convention oversized, or are the trucks oversized?

CLEAR: Pete plans to attend the oversize-truck convention.

Use hyphens in compound modifiers that come before nouns.

UNCLEAR: All right thinking parents worry about their kids' safety.

CLEAR: All right-thinking parents worry about their kids' safety.

Use hyphens when a few phrases modify one noun.

UNCLEAR: Rufus is a classic wine drinking, NPR listening, theater going Upper West Sider.

CLEAR: Rufus is a classic wine-drinking, NPR-listening, theater-going Upper West Sider.

Note that it's almost always correct to hyphenate before a noun and open up after a verb.

✓ The up-to-date gossip magazine thrilled Angel.

✓ The magazine, which was always up to date, thrilled Angel.

An easy way to remember when to use hyphens in age-related terms: if the word is *year*, hyphenate. If the word is *years*, do not. So you'd say *The two-year-old kid wailed*, but *The kid, who is two years old, wants some ice cream*.

ETHNICITY AND NATIONALITY

As nouns, compound ethnicities and nationalities may either be hyphenated (*African-American*, *Japanese-American*) or not hyphenated (*African American*, *Japanese American*). Whichever you choose, be sure to be consistent.

✓ Keith Gessen, a first-generation Russian American, has spent time in Moscow.

✓ In the 1920s and 30s, many African-Americans moved to the Northeast.

However, do hyphenate adjective forms that come before nouns.

✓ The Italian-American community soon embraced Tony Micelli as one of their own.

LETTERS AND NUMBERS

Use hyphens to separate numbers and letters.

✓ Harry's social security number is 023-12-3456.

✓ Just call 1-800-SARDINE.

✓ I am fed up! F-e-d-u-p!

ONE NOUN, TWO HYPHENS

If you're using the same noun in two hyphenated expressions, you may omit the noun from the first expression—but keep the hyphen, and be sure to include a space after it.

✓ The third- and fourth-string players looked dejected.

✓ The medal- and trophy-presenting ceremony took place on Tuesday.

VERBS AND PREPOSITIONS

Do not hyphenate phrases like *act up*.

UNDESIRABLE: I don't want to hold-up the proceedings.

✓ I don't want to hold up the proceedings.

UNDESIRABLE: It takes a while to settle-in to a new apartment.

✓ It takes a while to settle in to a new apartment.

IBID.

The Latin term *ibid.*, an abbreviation for *ibidem* ("in the same place"), is used in scholarly texts to cite the same source more than once consecutively. Traditionally, it has appeared in italics, but this is no longer necessary.

✓ During his only scene alone with Ophelia, Hamlet mocks her, verbally abuses her, and ultimately chases her away (Shakespeare, *Hamlet*, III.i.92–149). None of these prevent him from proclaiming, at her funeral, to have loved her more than "forty thousand brothers" (ibid., V.i.255).

I.E.

See E.G. vs. I.E.

ILLICIT

See ELICIT vs. ILLICIT.

ILLUSION

See ALLUSION vs. ILLUSION.

IMMIGRATE

See EMIGRATE vs. IMMIGRATE.

IMPLY vs. INFER

imply: to suggest indirectly

✓ Gertrude didn't mean to imply that Hamlet was nuts.

infer: to guess from evidence

✓ Because Hamlet behaved so strangely, people inferred that he was going nuts.

INDUCE

See DEDUCE vs. INDUCE.

INFER

See IMPLY vs. INFER.

–*ING* WORDS

The present participle form of English verbs ends in *-ing*. Its most basic use is to describe an action in progress, whether as part of a compound verb, an adjective, or in a participial phrase.

✓ She was humming and smiling at the sun when he walked up to the bench.

✓ We saw the running boy trip and fall, mere seconds before the bell rang.

✓ The ship sailing past us tooted its horn in welcome.

NOUNS

Gerunds are participles (*-ing* words) that are used as nouns.

✓ Eating cherries gives Alicia indigestion.

✓ One of Lila's duties is scrubbing the tiles.

DANGLING PARTICIPLES

Don't let your participle phrases dangle. If you're beginning a sentence with an *-ing* phrase, make sure that the phrase refers to whatever comes after it.

DANGLING: Racing for the phone, the martini glass shattered when Tina tripped.

The martini glass isn't racing; Tina is.

✓ Racing for the phone, Tina tripped and shattered the martini glass.

INTERJECTIONS

Interjections (words or phrases that convey emotion) are usually set off with punctuation of some kind. The interjections below are italicized.

✓ *Well*, what do you have to say for yourself?
✓ *You're kidding!* I'd never do that.
✓ *OK*, what do you suggest?
✓ Her essay was, *um*, less than wonderful.
✓ *Oh*, Mike, I don't know.

Some words exist only as interjections.

✓ *Whoops!* I dropped the vase.
✓ I got my report card—*ugh*.
✓ *Ssh*, don't forget you're in the library.

All kinds of words can be used as interjections.

✓ *Spike!* You're a bad dog.
✓ *And then*—hey, don't interrupt me.
✓ *Fool!*

IRRITATE

See AGGRAVATE VS. IRRITATE.

ITALICS

Italics refers to fonts where the letters slant to the right, *like so*. It is used to set off certain titles and emphasized expressions.

TITLES AND NAMES

Italicize the titles of novels, books, movies, and plays, and the names of newspapers, magazines, and journals.

✓ The *Village Voice* found *As Good As It Gets* jejune and boring.

Oh, and ships too!

✓ The *Nina*, the *Pinta*, and the *Santa Maria* sailed the ocean blue.

When making a title plural by adding *s*, do not italicize the *s*.

✓ The library has sixteen *Anna Karenina*s.

If the original title ends in *s*, keep it italicized in the plural.

✓ Brian sold sixteen *New York Times* in half an hour.

LEGAL CASES

Italicize the names of legal cases.

✓ The judge heard *Emmett v. Green* in March.

FOREIGN WORDS

Italicize words from foreign languages.

✓ Anyone who likes shrimp should try *mandu bok kum*.

Foreign words that are frequently used in English do not need to be italicized.

✓ "Ciao, dollface!" called the movie producer.

Do not italicize proper names from foreign languages.

✓ Every time Mike goes to the Prado, he checks out the Goyas.

WORDS AS WORDS

If you're referring to a word, rather than actually using that word as a grammatical part of your sentence, italicize it.

✓ Hector has always been baffled by the term *jumbo shrimp*.

Note that you can also put quotation marks around words used in this way, rather than italicizing them. Whichever method you choose, be consistent.

LETTERS

Italicize single letters.

✓ Rhoda triumphed with a six-letter word that included an *x* and a *q*.

✓ Pamela signs her name with a dramatic capital *P*.

Letter grades need not be italicized.

✓ You will never get an A.

EMPHASIS

Italics can be used to show emphasis.

✓ "I didn't say ice, I said *rice*," explained Maria.

> Use italics for emphasis as little as possible. Bold sentence structure and exciting word choice will make your writing dramatic; a bevy of italicized words will make it look amateurish.

MARKS FOLLOWING ITALICS

Only italicize titles and names themselves. Do not italicize punctuation marks, letters, or words that follow italicized titles and names.

✓ Tom, who just reread *The Talented Mr. Ripley*, is planning a trip to Italy.

✓ The *New Yorker*'s Ben McGrath wrote an article about knuckleball pitchers.

EMPHASIS ADDED

If you want to add emphasis to a quotation, italicize the words you wish to emphasize, and then add parentheses after the quotation in which you say "emphasis added," "italics mine," or something similar.

✓ Paine wrote, "Society in every state is a blessing, but government *even in its best state* is but a necessary evil" (emphasis mine).

IT'S VS. ITS

it's: contracted form of *it is*
✓ It's hard to dislike the prom queen.

its: possessive adjective corresponding to *it*
✓ The prom had wound its way to a close.

I VS. ME

Many people mix up the personal pronouns *I* and *me*. To avoid trouble, delete the other person from the equation and see what you're left with. If you've written *Sandra and me find that offensive*, take away *Sandra*. You're left with *Me find that offensive*. That sounds strange, so you know that *I*, not *me*, is correct.
✓ The giraffes took a liking to Ephraim and me.

JARGON

Avoid jargon whenever possible. Some people employ phrases like *leverage the research* and *optimize the content* because they believe, mistakenly, that jargon makes them sound smart. On the contrary, almost everyone glazes over in the presence of statements like *At the end of the day, our core competencies will mean the difference*. Unless the use of jargon will impress your boss and lead to a raise, stick to traditional words.

LATTER

See FORMER VS. LATTER.

LAY VS. LIE

Lay and *lie* are hard to get right. Remember, *lay* means "to place." *Lie* means "to recline."

✓ Watch carefully as I lay the rabbit on the table.

✓ As you can see, the rabbit will lie down on the table.

PAST TENSE

People confuse *lay* and *lie* because the past tense of *lie* is *lay*. If you memorize these two progressions, you'll have a much easier time keeping everything straight:

PRESENT	PAST	PAST PARTICIPLE
lay	laid	laid

✓ Now I have to lay this tomato on the cutting board.

✓ Yesterday, I laid a tomato on the cutting board.

✓ I had just laid the tomato down when you called.

PRESENT	PAST	PAST PARTICIPLE
lie	lay	lain

✓ I think I'll lie down for a while.

✓ Yesterday I lay awake instead of napping.

✓ I could have lain there fruitlessly, but instead I got up and vacuumed.

LESS VS. FEWER

When to use *less* and when to use *fewer*? There's an easy way to remember. If you can't count it, use *less*. If you can count it, use *fewer*.

✓ Cain has less love in his heart than anyone else I know.

✓ Cain gives fewer hugs than anyone else I know.

You can't count love, but you can count hugs.

LIE

See LAY VS. LIE.

LIKE VS. AS

Use *like*, not *as*, to compare unlike things.

✓ Her perfume smells like oranges.

✓ Henry, like Harold, enjoys rollerblading.

Only use *as* if you implying that the two things being compared are essentially the same. For instance, if you want to say that a certain performer appears in the garb of Elvis, you could use *as*.

✓ Betty sings as Elvis.

But if you want to suggest that Betty's singing resembles Elvis's, you are making a comparison, so *like* is the proper word.

✓ Betty sings like Elvis.

A few more examples:

✓ As a virgin, Mary was very surprised to discover that she was pregnant.

Mary *is* a virgin; use *as*.

✓ Like a virgin, Madonna is anxious about sleeping with her lover.

Madonna is not a virgin; she is only being compared to a virgin. Use *like*.

✓ Madonna is as giddy as a virgin.

As . . . as is a comparison formula. Essentially, Madonna's giddiness is the same as a virgin's giddiness. Since two identical things are being compared (two giddinesses), use *as*.

LISTS

Lists of three or more items are usually separated by a comma.

✓ Emma visited Morocco, Massachusetts, and Moscow, and came back with couscous, clam chowder, and cabbage.

✓ On Sunday mornings, Mrs. Duncan drives Billy to math circle, buys groceries for the week, returns clothing that didn't fit and buys more clothing, stops by the library, picks up Billy from math circle and drops him off at Johnny's house, visits her mother-in-law, and comes home to do the previous night's dishes—all before noon.

SEMICOLONS TO SEPARATE ITEMS

Semicolons may be used to separate the items in a list, especially if the list items include commas themselves, are complete sentences, or are simply very long.

✓ Billy is such a goody two-shoes: at home, he washes the dishes, sweeps the floor, and massages his mother's sore ankles, all without being asked; at school, he brings Mrs. Welty apples and always gets good grades; and on the playground, he never pinches other kids.

PARALLEL STRUCTURE

All items in your list should have the same grammatical form—all nouns, all gerunds, all prepositional phrases, all verb phrases, etc.

UNDESIRABLE: Swimming, biking, and ice cream are Olga's three favorite activities.

BETTER: Swimming, biking, and eating ice cream are Olga's three favorite activities.

BULLETED AND ENUMERATED LISTS

Some lists work best when each item sits on a separate line. You may choose to indent each entry and mark it with a bullet (•), a dash (—), or another symbol. Sometimes, it makes sense to enumerate the entries—with arabic numerals (1, 2, 3, . . .), roman numerals (I, II, III, . . .), or letters (A, B, C, . . . or a, b, c, . . .). Whatever presentation you choose, be sure to be consistent.

A satisfying list has parallel structure and thoughtful punctuation. For example, if you use periods to end entries, use them consistently to end each entry.

✓ The camp's welcome letter cheerfully insisted that Jenny pack the following:
- A flashlight.
- At least two bathing suits.
- A summer-reading book.
- Stamped postcards and pens.
- An index card with her home address.
- A water bottle.
- Bug spray.
- Sunscreen.
- At least two pairs of sneakers.
- A small backpack.

LOATH vs. LOATHE

loath: reluctant (*adj.*)
✓ Katie was loath to annoy her big brother.

loathe: to hate (*v.*)
✓ Secretly, she loathed him.

LOOSE vs. LOSE

loose: not fastened, relaxed (*adj.*)
✓ When the clasp on the watch became loose, Chester almost lost it.

lose: to misplace (*v.*)
✓ Chester worried he would lose his prized fob watch.

MARGINS

The *margins* are the white space that surround the text on a page.

JUSTIFICATION
Left-hand margins should be justified (each line should start at the same place). Right-hand margins need not be justified.

MARGIN MEASUREMENT
Left- and right-hand margins are usually 1.25 inches wide. Margins at the top and bottom of the page are usually 1 inch high. Margins smaller than 1 inch are undesirable.

SETTING MARGINS
In Microsoft Word, set margins by clicking on File and choosing Page Setup.

> Note to students: don't bother stretching your four-page paper into five pages by messing with the margins. Sure, it's easier than actually writing another page, but your teachers have seen a few papers in their day. They'll sense desperation and laziness as soon as they set eyes on those two-inch expanses of white bracketing your prose.

MAY BE vs. MAYBE

may be: is possible (*v.*)

✓ It may be that purple socks don't appeal to the ladies.

maybe: possibly (*adv.*)

✓ Maybe Parker should rethink his choice of socks.

ME

See I vs. Me.

MILITARY TERMS

MILITARY CONFLICTS

When they stand alone, words like *war*, *battle*, and so on should not be capitalized.

✓ With a loud shout, Mary plunged into the battle.

Do capitalize these words when they are part of the name of a conflict.

the American Revolution	the Revolution
the American War of Independence	the Revolutionary War
the Crusades	the Russian Revolution
the French Revolution	the Spanish-American War
the Gulf War	the Spanish Civil War
the Korean War	the Vietnam War
the Napoleonic War	the War of 1812
the First World War; World War I	the Great War
the Second World War	World War II

GROUPS AND ORGANIZATIONS

Nearly all names of military organizations, like nearly all military conflicts, are capitalized. Below, you'll find a partial list of major military groups.

the Allied forces	National Guard
Army Corps of Engineers	Pacific Fleet
Army Special Forces	Red Army
the Axis powers	Royal Air Force
the Central powers	Royal Canadian Mounted Police
Combined Chiefs of Staff	Royal Navy
Confederate army	United States Army
the French Resistance	United States Coast Guard
Green Berets	United States Marine Corps
Joint Chiefs of Staff	United States Navy
the Mounties	United States Signal Corps

When they stand alone, names of military forces need not be capitalized.

✓ I'm thinking of enlisting in the army.

✓ Men from the navy are in town for Fleet Week.

TIME

The military uses a twenty-four-hour time system. In this system, time is told with four digits and no colons or dots.

midnight:	2400 or 0000
noon:	1200
4:10 p.m.:	1610

When using the twenty-four-hour time system in a sentence, you may use the word *hours* after the four-digit number, use the abbreviation *h*, or simply use the four-digit number on its own.

✓ The camping trip will commence at 0900 hours.

✓ The camping trip will commence at 0900 h.

✓ The camping trip will commence at 0900.

TITLES

When military titles precede names, the titles should be capitalized.

✓ In a few minutes, Captain Cook will board the ship.

When military titles follow names, the titles should be lowercased.

✓ Cook, the feared captain, does not tolerate dissent.

Titles may be abbreviated only before a full name.

✓ On Friday nights, Sergeant Lopez goes to Bar None.

✓ On Friday nights, Sgt. Annalisa Lopez goes to Bar None.

SHIPS

Capitalize *and italicize* the names of ships.

✓ Hank pointed to his boat, the *Bella Luna*.

Do not italicize the abbreviations USS (United States ship) or HMS (Her/His Majesty's ship).

✓ By special invitation, Fiona boarded the HMS *Carnival*.

Do not use the word *ship* if you're also using USS or HMS.

✓ The USS *Constitution* is docked in Chicago.

MISPLACED MODIFIERS

A modifier, or modifying phrase, is a word or phrase that explains or describes a word. Misplaced modifiers are words, phrases, or clauses that do not point clearly to the word or words they modify.

MODIFIER MISPLACED: Like so many American men, the day came when Hank wanted a sports car.

Since *the day* is the subject, the sentence implies that *the day* is like *American men*. This is unintentionally funny and should be revised.

✓ Like so many American men, Hank eventually wanted a sports car.

✓ The day came when Hank, like so many American men, wanted a sports car.

MODIFIER MISPLACED: He is a short man with a bushy moustache weighing 200 pounds.

This sentence suggests that the man's moustache weighs 200 pounds.

✓ He is a short man weighing 200 pounds and sporting a bushy moustache.

✓ He is a short man with a bushy moustache, and he weighs 200 pounds.

To avoid misplacing your modifiers, make sure they're as close as possible to the word they are explaining or describing.

MODIFIER MISPLACED: I was told that Maurice broke the figurine by my mother.

✓ My mother told me that Maurice broke the figurine.

✓ I was told by my mother that Maurice broke the figurine.

Dangling participles obscure meaning in a similar way. Make sure your participle clauses are well placed.

DANGLING PARTICIPLE: Eating six corn dogs, nausea overwhelmed Jane.

This sentence suggests that *nausea* ate six corn dogs.

✓ Eating six corn dogs, Jane felt overwhelmed with nausea.

✓ Nausea overwhelmed Jane after she ate six corn dogs.

MISUSED WORDS

Some expressions are commonly used incorrectly because they sound like other combinations of words.

could of
>Should not be used instead of *could have*.

UNGRAMMATICAL: We could of made the squad if we'd practiced our back handsprings more.

GRAMMATICAL: We could have made the squad if we'd practiced our back handsprings more.

should of
>Should not be used instead of *should have*.

UNGRAMMATICAL: I guess I should of eaten something besides Twinkies.

GRAMMATICAL: I guess I should have eaten something besides Twinkies.

suppose to
>Should not be used instead of *supposed to*.

UNGRAMMATICAL: Hey, Mom said you're not suppose to eat the play-doh.

GRAMMATICAL: Hey, Mom said you're not supposed to eat the play-doh.

use to
>Should not be used instead of *used to*.

UNGRAMMATICAL: Marguerite use to do fifty pushups before breakfast.

GRAMMATICAL: Marguerite used to do fifty pushups before breakfast.

would of
>Should not be used instead of *would have*.

UNACCEPTABLE: Leo would of gone to the prom with Georgia if she'd asked him.

BETTER: Leo would have gone to the prom with Georgia if she'd asked him.

MIXED METAPHORS

A mixed metaphor occurs when you begin by comparing something to one thing and then shift and compare it to something else entirely.

MIXED METAPHOR: A bird in the hand is worth dodging bullets.

MIXED METAPHOR: Skulking like a shamed man, the great ship left the harbor, quiet as a mouse.

MIXED METAPHOR: Before plunging into the deep part of the pool, let's run through a few short examples.

If you tend to get carried away with metaphors, reread your work to make sure you've compared one thing to one other thing only.

MORAL vs. MORALE

moral: lesson; ethical belief

✓ Only Diana's strong moral sense prevented her from cheating.

morale: spirit

✓ When the temperature hit ninety-five, the morale of the volleyball team suffered.

NAMES AND TITLES

In general, capitalize people's names.

✓ At the Smiths' barbecue, I met Mrs. Patterson-Smith, Mary Alice Greensilverberg, and the Reverend José Rodriguez y Ortega.

Capitalize names that are abbreviated to one letter.

✓ The kids had a hard time pronouncing Mrs. Bresnahan's name, so she asked them to call her Mrs. B.

DE LA AND SIMILAR

The capitalization of names that include particles varies from case to case. Consider each such tricky name individually, and capitalize according to what's most commonly done. Note that some particles (*de*, *le*) are lowercased in the full name and uppercased when the last name is used alone.

✓ Daphne du Maurier attended the party; du Maurier drank a glass of champagne.

✓ Consuela rushed out to purchase the new John le Carré novel; she always bought Le Carré's novels in hardback.

FOLLOW PREFERENCE
Some people want their names spelled without capital letters; it's best to respect their lowercase wishes.

✓ Andrew fell asleep while studying the poetry of e. e. cummings.

MOM AND DAD
Don't capitalize family names unless they're being used in direct address or before a proper name.

✓ My mother and father still act like teenagers.

✓ Tina whined, "Can I, Mom? Pleeeeaaase?"

✓ Kenny visits his grandma every Tuesday.

✓ Kenny wrote a thank-you note to Grandma Rose.

TITLES
A person may have an academic title (*Ph.D.*), a professional title (*Col.*, *Atty.*), a social title (Mrs.), or a suffix (*Jr.*).

Professional titles precede a full name; academic titles follow a name. Social titles precede a name if there are no professional titles; suffixes follow a name.

ACADEMIC TITLES

Bachelor of Arts	B.A.
Doctor of Law	J.D.
Doctor of Medicine	M.D.
Doctor of Philosophy	Ph.D.
Master of Arts	M.A.
Master of Business Administration	M.B.A.
Master of Fine Arts	M.F.A.
Master of Science	M.S.

It's okay to omit the periods from the abbreviations above. *Ph.D.*, for example, can be written as *PhD*. The inclusion or exclusion of periods is a personal decision—omitting them is less conservative.

In sentences, academic titles that follow a name should be surrounded by commas.

✓ Jane Smith, M.B.A., wrote the best-selling *Your Money, Your Self*.

✓ Tina angled for an introduction to Doogie Howser, M.D., last night.

PROFESSIONAL TITLES

Ambassador	Amb.
Attorney	Attny.
Colonel	Col.
Doctor	Dr.
Father	Fr.
General	Gen.
Governor	Gov.
Honorable	Hon.
Monsignor	Msgr.
President	Pres.
Professor	Prof.
Representative	Rep.
Reverend	Rev.
Secretary	Sec.
Senator	Sen.
Sergeant	Sgt.
Treasurer	Treas.

The abbreviated titles above should be used only when both the first and last names are given (*Dr.* is the one exception).

✓ At noon, Sergeant Lopez reported for duty.

✓ At noon, Sgt. Annalisa Lopez reported for duty.

SOCIAL TITLES

Mr. is an appropriate social title for a man who does not have another professional title. The French equivalent is *M.* ("monsieur"). The plural of both *Mr.* and *M.* is *Messrs.* ("messieurs").

Ms. is an appropriate social title for a woman who does not have another professional title. Depending on context and on the preferences of the subject in question, you may also use *Miss* for an unmarried woman or *Mrs.* for a married woman. The French equivalents are *Mlle* ("mademoiselle") and *Mme* ("madame"); neither have a period. The plural of *Ms.*, *Miss*, *Mrs.*, and *Mme* is *Mmes.* ("mesdames"). The plural of *Mlle* is *Mlles* ("mesdemoiselles").

When one of these words comes before a proper name, those titles must be abbreviated.

✓ Mrs. Roberts is a hotshot lawyer.

When one of these words stands alone, it must be spelled out.

✓ Hey, Mister!

JR. AND SR.

The suffixes *Junior* and *Senior* should be abbreviated when used with names and spelled out when used alone.

✓ John F. Kennedy Jr. died in a plane crash.

✓ Duke Senior was unfairly banished by his usurping brother.

Commas surrounding *Jr.* and *Sr.* are optional these days. SparkNotes doesn't use them, but more traditional publishers sometimes do. Just be consistent.

OK: Martin Luther King, Jr., inspires Madeline.

ALSO OK: Jimmy Smith Sr. had a fight with his son.

NAUSEOUS vs. NAUSEATED

nauseous: inducing sickness or queasiness; describes the cause of nausea

✓ The nauseous journey made everyone green around the gills.

nauseated: feeling sick; describes the person experiencing the nausea

✓ As the boat thrashed through the waves, Jessica felt more and more nauseated.

NEITHER . . . NOR

See EITHER . . . OR, NEITHER . . . NOR.

NONEXISTENT WORDS

Some words, even words that you'll often hear people using, just don't exist according to the rules of good grammar. Here are some of the most commonly heard nonexistent words.

acrossed

UNACCEPTABLE: How are we supposed to get acrossed this river?

BETTER: How are we supposed to get across this river?

alot

UNACCEPTABLE: Sondra has alot of Xbox games.

BETTER: Sondra has a lot of Xbox games.

alright

UNACCEPTABLE: Stop yelling at him, alright?

BETTER: Stop yelling at him, all right?

anyways

UNACCEPTABLE: Anyways, what do you care?

BETTER: Anyway, what do you care?

a ways

UNACCEPTABLE: The bees live a ways toward the lake.

BETTER: The bees live a long way toward the lake.

drownded

UNACCEPTABLE: The ant drownded in the pool.

BETTER: The ant drowned in the pool.

everywheres

UNACCEPTABLE: Everywheres Jack looks, he sees Meg's face.

BETTER: Everywhere Jack looks, he sees Meg's face.

heighth

UNACCEPTABLE: In terms of breadth, depth, and heighth, Mr. Blunt has no equal.

BETTER: In terms of breadth, depth, and height, Mr. Blunt has no equal.

irregardless

UNACCEPTABLE: Colin decided to see the slasher flick irregardless of the terrible reviews it received.

BETTER: Colin decided to see the slasher flick regardless of the terrible reviews it received.

nowheres

UNACCEPTABLE: Loretta felt she had nowheres else to go.

BETTER: Loretta felt she had nowhere else to go.

somewheres

UNACCEPTABLE: Nina said the shoelace must be somewheres around here.

BETTER: Nina said the shoelace must be somewhere around here.

NUMBERS

COMMAS

When writing numbers, insert a comma after every three digits, starting from the right.

✓ After eating approximately 1,740 Skittles, Nanette looked a little pale.

✓ Each one of the 90,205 baseballs had to be signed by six o'clock.

If the number has a decimal point, start from the first digit to the left of the decimal point.

✓ Richie Rich spent every penny of his $1,000.01 monthly allowance on candy and video games.

Don't use commas with years or addresses.

DECIMALS

When writing decimals that are smaller than one, use a zero before the decimal point.

✓ Each question is worth approximately 0.5 point.

NUMBER RANGES

Use en dashes (–) to separate numbers in ranges.

✓ 1998–2000 were dark years for the abysmal football team.

✓ In October, the team lost 49–0.

✓ One problem was practice, which only ran 2 p.m.–2:30 p.m. one day per week.

If you're using an en dash, you don't need the words *from* or *between*.

✓ From 3 to 4, Emilie languished in detention.

✓ 3–4, Emilie languished in detention.

✓ This prom season, between May 2005 and June 2005, 6 million gowns were sold.

✓ This prom season, May 2005–June 2005, 6 million gowns were sold.

FRACTIONS

Spell out fractions.

✓ The raccoon made his way through three-fourths of the discarded pasta.

Use numerals for whole numbers and fractions.

✓ The obese cat weighed 16 ½ pounds.

Spelled-out fractions are almost always hyphenated. Omit the hyphen only when you're referring to the fraction as a separate entity, and not as part of something else.

✓ Gillian promised me exactly two-fifths of her birthday cake.

✓ I was disappointed because neither of the two fifths had a maraschino cherry.

LARGE NUMBERS

SparkNotes uses numerals for numbers in the thousands and spells out simple numbers in the millions and billions.

✓ More than 3,000 kids packed the auditorium.

✓ There must have been two million people watching the speech.

When fractions of large numbers are involved, we use numerals *and* spell out.

✓ According to my calculations, around 4.1 million ants have infested the house.

✓ The loft sold for a staggering $2.2 million.

MONEY

Here's the rule for writing about money: numerals go with signs, and spelled-out words go with spelled-out words.

✓ Everything in this store costs $1 or less.

✓ Everything in this store costs one dollar or less.

✓ Phil found 5€ on the street.

✓ Phil found five euros on the street.

ORDINALS

We at SparkNotes spell out ordinals under 100 and use numerals for ordinals over 100.

✓ The twenty-third time his mother told him to clean his room, Mike started to suspect she really meant it.

✓ On the 201st day of band camp, Yvette broke down.

PERCENT

Use numerals when referring to a percent.

✓ Almost 95 percent of the senior class plans to go to college in Florida.

✓ Victor answered only 50% of the multiple-choice questions correctly.

PLURALS

Make numbers plural as you would any other noun.

✓ The ones and twos are equally terrible years.

There is no need to include an apostrophe before the s when making numerals plural. Simply add an s.

✓ Babs is going to throw a 1990s theme party.

✓ Henrietta hoped to score in the high 90s on the anatomy quiz.

ROMAN NUMERALS

Use roman numerals as little as possible. Arabic numbers (1, 2, 3, and so on) or their spelled-out versions are easier to understand quickly.

ARABIC	ROMAN
1	I
5	V
10	X
50	L

ARABIC	ROMAN
100	C
500	D
1,000	M

Adding a smaller roman numeral to the left of a numeral makes the number smaller. For example, 4 is written *IV*. Adding a smaller roman numeral to the right of a numeral makes the number larger. For example, 15 is written *XV*.

SPELLING OUT NUMBERS

Our suggestions for when to spell out numbers and when to use numerals vary depending on the text in question. If you're working on a very technical paper, you may want to use numerals for all numbers. If you're working on a more chatty text, you may want to spell out numbers from one to ten. SparkNotes spells out numbers from zero to one hundred. Whichever method you choose, be sure to stay consistent. And we also spell out any number that starts a sentence.

✓ For his ninety-ninth birthday, Andrew wanted expensive cigars.

✓ One hundred and fifty years ago, a time machine was made.

We at SparkNotes use numerals for numbers over one hundred.

✓ I have tripped over that rug approximately 3,237 times.

Spell out numbers mentioned in dialogue.

✓ Justin said, "I've turned her down at least three hundred times."

Always use numerals in charts and tables.

If you're dealing with several numbers in one sentence, it's okay to bend your own rules to avoid awkwardness.

ODD: One resident turned eighty, another turned ninety-one, and another turned 101.

BETTER: One resident turned eighty, another turned ninety-one, and another turned one hundred and one.

It's also okay to use numerals if your instincts are crying out for them—if you're talking about a shoe size, for instance. There are no hard-and-fast rules about when to make exceptions; you just have to go with your gut.

AWKWARD: The Falcon was a one-hundred-and-seventy-nine-kilowatt engine.

LESS AWKWARD: The Falcon was a 179-kilowatt engine.

TELEPHONE NUMBERS

There are several ways to write telephone numbers. One option is to separate the numbers with hyphens.

✓ Call Ariel's Deli at 212-233-4561.

Another option is to enclose the area code in parentheses and separate the other two sets of numbers with a hyphen.

✓ Call Ariel's Deli at (212) 233-4561 if you want to order pickles for delivery.

If you like, you can include the numeral 1 before area codes. This is often done with toll-free numbers.

✓ I called 1-800-333-2222 and ordered patriotic popcorn.

Many companies spell out words in their phone numbers by replacing numerals with corresponding letters from the number pad. The idea is that consumers will remember words more easily than they will remember numbers. In writing, these words should be spelled out in capital letters.

✓ Brint called (617) 333-FILM to find out where *Wet Hot American Summer* was playing.

TIME

If you use *o'clock*, you must spell out the time.

✓ Every day at six o'clock, I eat crackers and cheese.

If you use *a.m.* or *p.m.*, there's no need to write *in the morning* or *at night*.

✓ Waking up before ten a.m. is almost impossible for Harold.
✓ Waking up before ten in the morning is almost impossible for Harold

Use numerals if you want to stress a precise time.

✓ The test will begin promptly at 8:20 a.m.

See MILITARY TERMS for questions on the twenty-four-hour clock.

ONE ANOTHER

See EACH OTHER vs. ONE ANOTHER.

OPINIONS

In most formal papers, the word *I* should not appear. Simply assert your opinions instead of identifying them as opinions.

UNDESIRABLE: I think *Fahrenheit 451* is terrifying.

DESIRABLE: The world depicted in *Fahrenheit 451* is a terrifying one.

ORDINAL NUMBERS

See NUMBERS.

PARALLEL STRUCTURE

Sentences must have parallel structure. That is, they must start, continue, and end in the same way.

LISTS

It's especially common to find errors of parallelism in sentences that list actions or items. If you list two gerunds, don't switch and list a noun; if you list two nouns, don't switch and list a phrase; and so on.

UGLY: Porter never liked drinking wine, eating cheese, or cocktail parties.

✓ Porter never liked drinking wine, eating cheese, or going to cocktail parties.

✓ Porter never liked wine, cheese, or cocktail parties.

AWKWARD: The car is sleek, fast, and exhilarates whoever drives it.

✓ The car is red, sleek, fast, and exhilarating.

If you're writing a list in which the first item is preceded by a preposition or an article, be consistent with the rest of the list. Either leave out the following prepositions/articles (it's allowed) or include the prepositions/articles before every item.

✓ Todd's mother told him that he was irresponsible, unthinking, and smug.

✓ Todd's mother told him that he was irresponsible, that he was unthinking, and that he was smug.

EITHER . . . OR AND COMPANY

Watch out for errors of parallelism when you use *either . . . or, neither . . . nor, both . . . and, not only . . . but also.* The words on either side of those equations must use parallel structure.

AWKWARD: Not only did you insult me, but also my mother.

✓ Not only did you insult me, but you also insulted my mother.

✓ You insulted not only me but also my mother.

PARENTHESES

Parentheses are used to separate off asides or nonessential information. Material set off by commas and dashes should be pertinent to the rest of the sentence; material enclosed by parentheses can be a little more discursive.

✓ That man (the one in the baseball cap) just asked for my number.

> Parentheses set off information more firmly than commas or dashes do. They tell the reader, "It's okay to skip this if you like." Dashes insist, "Pause here and read this!" Commas say, meekly, "A pause would be nice."

Parentheses are used to cite sources.

✓ In the next paragraph, he writes, "Some people show evil as a great race horse shows breeding" (Hemingway, 109).

Parentheses can be used to provide translations or short explanations next to rare terms.

✓ Carl called me a *jabroni* (loser).

Do not italicize parentheses that enclose an italicized word.

✓ The formal *you* (*vous*) has confused students for years.

PHONE NUMBERS

Parentheses can be used around area codes.

✓ If you want the best wallpaper in town, call (212) 633-2222.

WITH PERIODS

If parenthetical matter is included in a sentence, closing punctuation should go outside the parentheses. This holds true even if the parentheses enclose a complete sentence.

✓ Sheldron refused to invite him (they've been enemies since first grade).

Parenthetical expressions that stand alone and are complete sentences get their own punctuation.

✓ Seymour has never been to Italy. (In fact, he's never left the country.)

WITH COMMAS, SEMICOLONS, COLONS

You should never place commas, semicolons, or colons before closing parentheses; always put them outside closing parentheses.

✓ Whatever you do (and really, I don't care), don't get me involved.

✓ She bid adieu to Sandy (her parrot); then, with a sigh, she turned away.

✓ She listed several options (all of them tempting): mint, chocolate, and raspberry.

WITH QUESTION MARKS OR EXCLAMATION POINTS

Don't place question marks or exclamation points before closing parentheses unless they are part of the parenthetical material.

✓ Who better to herd sheep than Nate (the one in the cloak)?

The question mark is part of the sentence, not part of the parenthetical.

✓ Neha was wondering (weren't we all?) when the pigs would arrive.

The question mark is part of the parenthetical, not part of the sentence.

✓ The package didn't arrive, but don't tell Sheila (or anyone else)!

The exclamation point is part of the sentence, not part of the parenthetical.

✓ The package arrived (finally!) after five weeks.

The exclamation point is part of the parenthetical, not part of the sentence.

PARENTHESES WITHIN PARENTHESES

For parentheses within parentheses, use either brackets or parentheses; whichever you choose, be consistent.

✓ Mrs. Whelan refused to let her daughter date Reg (she hated his sneering [shockingly rude, really] attitude).

✓ Mrs. Whelan forbid her daughter to date Reg (she hated his sneering (shockingly rude, really) attitude).

PASSIVE VOICE

Passive voice refers to a sentence whose subject *is being acted upon*.

PASSIVE: The chicken was chased by Mike.

PASSIVE: Frank's head is surrounded by bristly hair.

In the active voice, the subject acts.

ACTIVE: Mike chased the chicken.

ACTIVE: Bristly hair surrounds Frank's head.

Use the active voice instead of the passive voice whenever possible. The passive voice will make your writing dull and listless; the active voice, which allows you to use strong, interesting verbs, will make your writing lively.

Passive voice is appropriate when the agent performing the action is unknown or irrelevant.

✓ The chicken had already been plucked and cleaned by the time Mike returned to the farm on Tuesday.

PEAK vs. PIQUE

peak: the top of something (*n.*)

✓ At the peak of his success, the rock star often trashed hotel rooms.

pique: to excite (*v.*); wounded vanity (*n.*)

✓ Once, in a pique, he defenestrated a microfridge, nearly smashing a reporter's face.

✓ The VH1 special piqued Marly's interest in debauched rock stars.

PERIODS

A period (.) marks the end of a sentence.

ABBREVIATIONS
Use periods to mark words that have been abbreviated.

✓ Meghan, a.k.a. Nemesis No. One, just strode into the cafeteria.

WITH QUOTATIONS
Place periods before closing quotation marks at the end of a sentence.

✓ "If we pitch the tent here," Christian said, "we'll avoid the bears."

✓ As Oscar Wilde put it, Philadelphia is "dreadfully provincial."

SPACES AFTER PERIODS
Nearly every book, magazine, and newspaper you'll ever come across uses one space, not two, after periods. Some teachers ask their students to use two spaces after periods; if you're after good grades, you should respect their two-space wishes.

UNDESIRABLE: Mrs. Snippet requires two spaces after periods. It's a shame.

DESIRABLE: Ms. Schazz prefers one space. She says it looks better.

QUOTATIONS
When quoting material, do not place a period before the closing quotation marks unless that period occurs in the original text.

✓ As Oscar Wilde put it, Philadelphia is "dreadfully provincial" ("The American Invasion").

PHASE

See FAZE VS. PHASE.

PIQUE

See PEAK VS. PIQUE.

PLACE NAMES

ADDRESSES

When writing addresses, use commas to separate street from town and town from state.

✓ When we first settled at 60 Mirror Lane, Darkling, Mississippi, we didn't know the house was haunted.

CAPITALIZATION

Here's the easy rule about capitalizing place names: if it appears on a map, it should be capitalized. Regions, states, cities, streets, highways, parks, buildings, monuments, mountains, rivers, coasts—capitalize all of them.

✓ The Pacific Northwest suits Justin's temperament.

Nicknames for places usually get capitalized.

✓ Shane romanticizes the Wild West, but in truth he's a city boy to his core.

✓ Tristan plans to live on the Cape for the summer and make money waiting tables.

STATES

When writing the name of a city and a state, surround the state with commas if it's an abbreviation.

✓ Maggie goes to Boston, Mass., whenever she craves clam chowder.

In formal writing, states' names should be spelled out.

✓ I lost my heart in New York, New York.

STATE ABBREVIATIONS

There are two systems for abbreviating state names. The first uses lower-case letters and periods: Minn. for Minnesota, N.Y. for New York. The second is the two-capital-letter system used by the post office: MN and

NY. Either system is fine, although only the second should be used when postal addresses are involved.

Alabama	Ala.	AL
Alaska	Alaska	AK
Arizona	Ariz.	AZ
Arkansas	Ark.	AR
California	Cal., Calif.	CA
Colorado	Col., Colo.	CO
Connecticut	Conn.	CT
Delaware	Del.	DE
District of Columbia	D.C.	DC
Florida	Fla.	FL
Georgia	Ga.	GA
Hawaii	Hawaii, H.I.	HI
Idaho	Ida., Id.	ID
Illinois	Ill.	IL
Indiana	Ind.	IN
Iowa	Iowa, Ia.	IA
Kansas	Kan., Kans.	KS
Kentucky	Ken., Ky.	KY
Louisiana	La.	LA
Maine	Me.	ME
Maryland	Md.	MD
Massachusetts	Mass.	MA
Michigan	Mich.	MI
Minnesota	Minn.	MN
Mississippi	Miss.	MS
Missouri	Mo.	MO
Montana	Mont.	MT
Nebraska	Neb., Nebr.	NE
Nevada	Nev.	NV
New Hampshire	N.H.	NH
New Jersey	N.J.	NJ
New Mexico	N.M., N.Mex.	NM
New York	N.Y.	NY
North Carolina	N.C.	NC
North Dakota	N.D., N.Dak.	ND
Ohio	Ohio	OH
Oklahoma	Okla., Ok.	OK
Oregon	Ore.	OR
Pennsylvania	Penna., Penn., Pa.	PA
Puerto Rico	P.R.	PR
Rhode Island	R.I.	RI
South Carolina	S.C.	SC
South Dakota	S.D., S.Dak.	SD
Tennessee	Tenn	TN

Texas	Tex.	TX
Utah	Utah, Ut.	UT
Vermont	Vt.	VT
Virginia	Va.	VA
(U.S.) Virgin Islands	U.S.V.I., V.I.	VI
Washington	Wash.	WA
West Virginia	W.Va.	WV
Wisconsin	Wis., Wisc.	WI
Wyoming	Wyo.	WY

PLAGIARISM

Plagiarism—presenting someone else's work as your own—rears its ugly head in many forms. Everyone knows that paying someone to write your college application essay is illegal; everyone knows that copying an online article on *The Scarlet Letter* is unethical. And most people realize that lifting a sentence or two verbatim from a couple of different encyclopedias and stringing them together is extremely fishy.

But plagiarism also includes taking credit for other people's ideas, not just their words.

Say you are poking around online, doing research for a paper on Hemingway and nature. You find an article that makes a great point about rabbits in *For Whom the Bell Tolls*—great because it's useful for your argument. The text reads:

> The association of the band of fighters with rabbits underscores their fragile position relative to the Fascists. Like rabbits, Robert Jordan and his band live in close contact with the natural world: they are a small and vulnerable group, in sharp contrast to the Fascists and their threatening industrial war machinery.

You rejoice and triumphantly type into your document, "The rabbits in *For Whom the Bell Tolls* are vulnerable natural creatures, much like Robert Jordan and his friends." Uh-oh. Although the only important word you've copied is *vulnerable*, the main idea in your sentence is the comparison between Robert Jordan and the rabbits, and this comparison is not yours. It comes directly from the article you found online. Unless you give the writer credit for the idea, you'll be committing plagiarism.

For more on how to give credit where credit is due, see FOOTNOTES AND ENDNOTES and CITATIONS IN TEXT.

PLURALS

In general, noun plurals are formed by adding *s* or *es*. A final *y* changes to *ies*.

PROPER NOUNS

Form the plural with proper nouns simply by adding *s* or *es*. Note that there is no need for an apostrophe.

✓ Two New Yorks existed: one for the rich, and one for the poor.

When forming the plural of a name like *Suzy*, simply add *s*. Don't change the *y* to *ies*, since doing so changes the original word.

✓ How many Suzys are there in the fourth grade?

Use *s* or *es* alone, without an apostrophe, when forming the plural of a family.

✓ The Waxes bring Mrs. Wax's famous brownies wherever they go.

LETTERS

To make an uppercase letter used as a word plural, add an *s*.

✓ Marvin's six Cs did not please his father.

To make an italicized lowercase letter used as a word plural, add an *s*.

✓ Yael won the tic-tac-toe game with a flurry of *x*s.

NUMERALS

There is no need to include an apostrophe before the *s* when making numerals plural. Simply add an *s*.

✓ In the 1980s, Cabbage Patch dolls were all the rage.

✓ There are three 1s in 12113.

QUOTATIONS

To make a quoted phrase plural, add an apostrophe plus *s* inside the quotation marks.

✓ Cal answered with a flurry of "I'm so sorry's" and "Please forgive me's."

ABBREVIATIONS

Make capitalized abbreviations plural by simply adding an *s*.

✓ The three POWs were conducted to the base camp.

Make most truncated or letters-omitted abbreviations plural by adding an *s* before the period.

✓ We invited both the Drs. Brown, father and son.

To make plural an abbreviation that has two or more periods, use an apostrophe and *s*.

✓ The Ph.D.'s at the party are likely to be either stuffy or smelly.

TRICKY PLURALS

Some plurals are tricky, but the application of common sense will do the trick in most cases. For example, is *mother-in-laws* or *mothers-in-law* correct? We're talking about more than one mother, not more than one law, so the latter is right. When in doubt, consult a dictionary.

✓ Bruce and Benny faced courts-martial.

SILENT *S*

If a word ends in an unpronounced *s*, make it plural by ignoring it— don't add an *s*, an apostrophe, or anything else.

✓ Strangely enough, there were three François in Mrs. Apple's class.

POLITICAL TERMS

See CULTURAL TERMS.

PORE VS. POUR

pore: to read attentively (*v.*); skin opening (*n.*)

✓ Zack pored over his teacher's scribbled comments.

pour: to dispense liquid (*v.*)

✓ Chad poured himself a large glass of orange juice.

PREPOSITIONS

AT THE END OF A SENTENCE

At some point, you probably heard that it's incorrect to end sentences with prepositions (words like *of*, *for*, *with*, *at*, *to*, *in*, *from*, *up*, and so on). But many people think it's okay to break this rule. In fact, occasionally you'll come across a sentence that would sound painfully awkward if it *didn't* end in a preposition.

AWKWARD: From where in the world did you come?

LESS AWKWARD: Where in the world did you come from?

AWKWARD: Janine is the meanest girl on whom I have ever laid eyes.

LESS AWKWARD: Janine is the meanest girl I have ever laid eyes on.

AWKWARD: We have much for which to be thankful.

LESS AWKWARD: We have much to be thankful for.

IDIOMATIC USE

Almost nothing drives nonnative speakers of English crazier than the task of matching prepositions with words—and native speakers don't exactly have an easy time of it, either. Logic won't help you, since most word-preposition pairs are a matter of tradition. Memorization is the key. Here is a partial list of some common pairs:

✓ He can't *abide by* the no-spitting rule.

✓ He was *accompanied by* an angry model.

✓ How do you *account for* the state of your bedroom?

✓ She *accused me* of stealing her feather boa.

✓ The principal *acquitted* her *of* all wrongdoing.

✓ I am *adept at* fooling principals.

✓ I am even more *adept in* the art of fooling vice principals.

✓ I *agreed to* eat the broccoli.

✓ She is *anxious about* her organic chemistry exam.

✓ He *apologized for* losing the hamsters in the heating vent.

✓ She *applied for* a credit card.

✓ My mother pretends to *approve of* my boyfriend.

✓ I *arrived at* work around noon.

- ✓ You *believe in* ghosts.
- ✓ I can't be *blamed for* your neuroses.
- ✓ Do you *care about* me?
- ✓ The intervention *centers on* your wild binges.
- ✓ He's in *charge of* grocery shopping.
- ✓ The shout *coincided with* a loud crash.
- ✓ Nothing *compares to* you.
- ✓ *Compared with* her, you're a movie star.
- ✓ What is there to *complain about*?
- ✓ If you don't *comply with* the ban on gum, you'll be banished to detention.
- ✓ I never *confide in* her.
- ✓ *Confiding* your secrets *to* her is like emailing them to the entire class.
- ✓ Ice cream *consists of* milk, fat, and sugar.
- ✓ He can always *count on* money from his mommy.
- ✓ I *depend on* no one.
- ✓ That's where cats *differ from* dogs.
- ✓ She *differs with* him on the matter of cilantro.
- ✓ Screeching is *different from* singing.
- ✓ It's terrible to *discriminate against* parakeets.
- ✓ He is completely *enamored of* the exchange student.
- ✓ I have a plan to *escape from* this prison.
- ✓ There's no *excuse for* your behavior.
- ✓ You can't *hide from* your past.
- ✓ It was all he'd *hoped for*.
- ✓ I hate to *impose on* you, but could I borrow your car?
- ✓ She was finally *independent of* her mother.
- ✓ I must *insist upon* it.
- ✓ He *instilled* his passion for the Red Sox *in* his son.
- ✓ Her *mastery of* table tennis is remarkable.
- ✓ Her *mastery over* all other competitors is indisputable.
- ✓ It's impossible to *object to* her lucid arguments.
- ✓ *Pray for* me.
- ✓ I refuse to *participate in* this discussion.
- ✓ *Protect* me *from* evil.
- ✓ *Provide* me *with* plenty of Skittles.
- ✓ She *reconciled with* her best friend.

- ✓ She *reconciled* herself *to* the idea that she'd never trust Sally again.
- ✓ She stayed home to *recover from* the flu.
- ✓ I *rely on* myself.
- ✓ She *stared at* his chest.
- ✓ He *subscribes to* several trashy magazines.
- ✓ I *succeeded in* fooling him.
- ✓ *Wait for* me!
- ✓ *Work with* me!

TWO PREPOSITIONS

Try not to place two prepositions right next to each other in a sentence. Rewrite to avoid this awkward syntax.

AWKWARD: Francesca just walked by, by the way.

LESS AWKWARD: By the way, Francesca just walked by.

PRONOUNS

PRONOUN AGREEMENT

The rule governing pronoun agreement is a simple one: if the noun is plural, the pronoun that replaces it should be plural. If the noun is singular, the pronoun that replaces it should be singular. In the following sentences, the nouns and pronouns are italicized.

- ✓ The *boys* had planned to go skinny dipping, but *their* courage failed them.
- ✓ *Martina* didn't have a good time at *her* party.

For a detailed explanation of the thorny pronoun issues surrounding gender, see GENDERED LANGUAGE.

PRONOUN SHIFT

Be careful not to shift pronouns mid-sentence or mid-paragraph. If you start by using *you* (or *one*, or *I*, etc.), keep on using *you*.

SHIFTY: When one goes shopping, be careful not to lose your wallet.

- ✓ When one goes shopping, one should be careful not to lose one's wallet.
- ✓ When you go shopping, be careful not to lose your wallet.

PRONOUN AMBIGUITY

Be sure to avoid deploying pronouns in ambiguous ways. Rewriting sentences is usually the best way to stamp out ambiguity.

AMBIGUOUS: Yesterday, Sarah and Emma talked about her strong dislike of blue cheese.

CLEAR: Sarah strongly dislikes blue cheese, as she told Emma yesterday.

Occasionally, you'll have to repeat a proper name instead of using a pronoun. This may sound a little awkward, but it's better than being unclear.

AMBIGUOUS: The Patriots and the Vikings both assumed they would prevail, and, sure enough, they won.

CLEAR: The Patriots and the Vikings both assumed they would prevail, and, sure enough, the Patriots won.

PROPHESY VS. PROPHECY

prophesy: to predict (*v.*)

✓ Vlad prophesied many torrid romances in my future.

prophecy: a prediction (*n.*)

✓ I hope Vlad's prophecies are accurate.

PROSCRIBE VS. PRESCRIBE

proscribe: to prohibit

✓ A new rule proscribed extremely short skirts.

prescribe: to give a remedy

✓ Unimpressed by Boris's moaning, the school nurse prescribed an aspirin and a quick return to class.

QUALIFIERS

Avoid qualifying your assertions with phrases like *rather, quite, kind of, sort of*, and so on. Qualifiers make your writing sound namby-pamby.

WEAK: In *Frankenstein*, Shelley kind of suggests that men almost disregard the desires of women.

STRONGER: In *Frankenstein*, Shelley suggests that men often disregard the desires of women.

> You should strive to be nuanced and thoughtful in your writing. But filling your prose (or your speech) with junk like *This rather shocking piece is sort of the antithesis of Crewdson's original project* is not the way to do it. People want to use qualifying phrases (*rather, sort of*, etc.) to hedge their bets or to prove that their argument is complex. In fact, qualifiers dilute the power of your argument. Show your readers the refinement of your thinking by putting together a series of strong sentences that express that refinement, not by hemming and hawing.

QUESTION MARKS

A question mark (?) comes at the end of an interrogative sentence. Aren't question marks lovely and curvaceous?

INDIRECT QUESTIONS

Never, ever use question marks with indirect questions. (And never, ever put quotation marks around indirect questions.)

✓ Izzy demanded to know why Parker looked so guilty.

✓ Who stole Dani's jellies is the question.

These rules apply even when the indirect question consists of only one word. If you like, you can italicize one-word indirect questions.

✓ Someone had done it. The question plaguing everyone was *who*.

IN SENTENCES

When writing a direct question in another sentence, use a comma before the question and a question mark after it. Note that quotation marks are *not* required; neither is a capital letter at the beginning of the question.

✓ Sometimes I wonder, do squirrels find all the nuts they bury?

✓ If someone says, what kind of accent do you have? one more time, I'm going to explode.

QUOTATIONS

Short quotations should be preceded by a comma. (Note that *short* usually means around three lines of text or poetry.)

✓ It was then that she said, "Do as you please. I wash my hands of you."

Omit the introductory comma if the quotation fits grammatically into the sentence.

✓ Micheldene claimed that "outside every fat man there was an even fatter man trying to close in."

Longish quotations are often introduced by a colon.

✓ Benjamin Franklin offers witty advice on how to ferret out a woman's faults: "I am about courting a girl I have had but little acquaintance with. How shall I come to a knowledge of her faults, and whether she has the virtues I imagine she has? *Answer*. Commend her among her female acquaintance."

Always place question marks, exclamation points, semicolons, and colons outside closing quotation marks—unless they are part of the original quotation.

✓ How can you question the genius of Led Zepplin's immortal words, "Oh oh oh oh oh, you don't have to go"?

The speaker is asking the question, so the question mark goes outside the quotation marks.

✓ Then Antony cries, "Fie, wrangling queen!"

In this instance, the exclamation point is part of the original quotation.

LONG QUOTATIONS

Long quotations are usually *set off* (started on a new line, indented, sometimes set in a smaller or different font than the regular text, and sometimes spaced closer between lines than the regular text). Long quotations may also be *run in* (enclosed in quotation marks and formatted as part of the regular text, as short quotations are).

Quotations longer than one hundred words should be set off; so should poetry and quotations that are longer than one paragraph.

✓ Wilde's story "The Remarkable Rocket" begins in classic fairy-tale style.

> The King's son was going to be married, so there were general rejoicings. He had waited a whole year for his bride, and at last she had arrived. She was a Russian Princess, and had driven all the way from Finland in a sledge drawn by six reindeer. The sledge was shaped like a great golden swan, and between the swan's wings lay the little Princess herself. Her long ermine cloak reached right down to her feet, on her head was a tiny cap of silver tissue, and she was as pale as the Snow Palace in which she had always lived. So pale was she that as she drove through the streets all the people wondered. "She is like a white rose!" they cried, and they threw down flowers on her from the balconies.
>
> At the gate of the Castle the Prince was waiting to receive her. He had dreamy violet eyes, and his hair was like fine gold. When he saw her he sank upon one knee, and kissed her hand.

LONG DIALOGUE

If one character or person's dialogue goes on for more than one paragraph, it is common to include opening quotation marks before each new paragraph. Only the last paragraph gets closing quotation marks.

✓ With a modest smile, Bobby said, "When I first arrived, I dreamed of starring in a Broadway show. And sure enough, I got a great part after just two auditions.
"Of course, I happen to be stunningly beautiful and unbelievably talented."

POETRY

Quotations of three or more lines of poetry should be set off from the main text.

✓ In his poem "Heaven," Rupert Brooke writes,

> Fish say, they have their Stream and Pond;
> But is there anything Beyond?
> This life cannot be All, they swear,
> For how unpleasant, if it were!

If you're quoting two lines of poetry, you can run them in. In this case, separate the lines with slashes. Put spaces on either side of the slashes.

✓ Brooke gently satirizes the human predicament with the lines, "Fish say, they have their Stream and Pond; / But is there anything Beyond?"

QUOTATIONS WITHIN QUOTATIONS

If a run-in quotation itself contains words in quotation marks, use single quotation marks around those words.

✓ The breathless narrator exclaims, "Jack said, 'You're pretty,' and I practically fainted. Then he said, 'I like your shoes'!"

In set-off quotations, which are not surrounded by quotation marks, use double quotation marks around quoted material.

✓ The breathless narrator delivers a nearly hysterical description of her day:

> Jack said, "You're pretty," and I practically fainted. Then he said, "I like your shoes"!

OMITTING TEXT

To omit part of a sentence from quoted material, replace the sentence with three ellipsis dots separated on all sides by spaces.

✓ Bertie muses, "Well . . . when a girl suddenly asks you out of the clear blue sky if you don't sometimes feel that the stars are God's daisy-chain, you begin to think a bit."

To omit a sentence or sentences from quoted material, replace the deleted material with four ellipsis dots. Don't insert a space before the first dot (the first dot functions as the period); do insert spaces between the following three.

✓ Bertie is sure we'll agree: "You know how it is with some girls. . . . There is something about their personality that paralyses the vocal cords and reduces the contents of the brain to cauliflower."

Indicate the omission of a paragraph (and a full sentence; see below) with four ellipsis points before the omitted paragraph.

✓ In Chapter 4, Bertie's aunt pays him a visit.

> It has been well said of Bertram Wooster that, while no one views his flesh and blood with a keener and more remorselessly critical eye, he is nevertheless a man who delights in giving credit where credit is due. And if you have followed these memoirs of mine with the proper care, you will be aware that I have frequently had occasion to emphasise the fact that Aunt Dahlia is all right. . . .
> This being so, you may conceive of my astonishment at finding her at my bedside at such an hour.

There is no need to use ellipses at the beginning or end of sentences, even if you're starting to quote in the middle of a sentence or stopping before the end of one. Just plunge in or stop abruptly, with no fussing over ellipses.

✓ Wodehouse writes, "I know, because I wear them myself, and I am a singularly romantic figure."

✓ Bertie describes him as "one of those freaks you come across from time to time during life's journey who can't stand London."

Respect the author's original marks. It's fine to retain commas from the original sentence, and to place question marks, exclamation points, etc., after three ellipsis dots if they come at the end of the original sentence.

✓ Callahan says, "Teach your child respect for himself and others, . . . and you'll be doing the best you can."

✓ He writes, "Have you ever considered the latent possibilities for dramatic situations . . . ?"

EMENDING TEXT

When quoting material, it's okay to place periods and commas before the closing quotation marks even if those marks don't occur in the original text. It's also fine to replace a comma from the original text with a period if that works better for your sentence, and vice versa.

✓ In a letter, Henry James wrote, "It's a complex fate, being an American."

The basic rule: unless you're quoting legal material or working under unusually formal circumstances, you're allowed to change capitals to lowercase letters and vice versa. There is no need to bracket the changed letter to show that you've changed it.

✓ Angry about his early bedtime, Dane cursed his mother with a cry of "fie, wrangling queen!"

Fie, which is capitalized in the original, has been lowercased.

✓ Wodehouse expresses my feelings precisely: "If you want to get me out of New York, you will have to use dynamite."

If, which is lowercased in the original, has been uppercased.

You can also lowercase the first word of a set-off quotation if your sentence structure calls for it.

✓ After the first mysterious groan sounded,

> a solemn silence ensued, and marks of fear were visible upon all three faces . . .

FORMAL STYLE

In legal contexts and some very formal writing, you might want to bracket capital letters you've changed to lowercase, and vice versa.

✓ The contract stipulates that the manuscript will be delivered "[n]o later than August 1, 2007."

A very formal method of quotation requires you to place periods and commas outside closing quotation marks if those marks don't occur in the original text. This method is used in Britain much more than it is in America. It may be required in some American universities or for some scholarly works.

✓ In a letter, Henry James wrote, "It's a complex fate, being an American".

GRAMMATICAL INCORPORATION

Don't use quoting as an excuse to lose control of grammar. Quotations *must* fit grammatically into your text.

✓ The critic suggests that the murderer's "cunning . . . in combination with his bravado" led to his success.

Be sure that your text still makes sense after you've omitted parts of a quotation. Don't allow any stray phrases or incomplete sentences to slip in.

✓ Wallace asserts that "Mr. Updike . . . has for years been constructing protagonists who are basically all the same guy . . . and who are all clearly stand-ins for the author himself."

In particular, make sure your own tense and the tense of the quoted material match up. The best way to do this is to choose your quoted material carefully, avoiding any unwanted tenses. Ideally, you can avoid the problem altogether.

✓ No one can stand Daniel. Like Austen's Mr. Collins, he isn't "a sensible man" and "the deficiency of nature" hasn't been remedied "by education or society."

If you simply can't work around the problem, it's okay to change the text and bracket your changes. Use this device as little as possible.

✓ Like Galsworthy's character, he enjoys a privileged childhood and "[has] never heard his father or his mother speak in an angry voice, either to each other, himself, or anybody else."

SIC

The word *sic*, in brackets, can be inserted to show that a grammatical mistake or a misspelling is the author's fault, not yours. Try to avoid the use of *sic*, however; it's snotty and makes you sound scornful. It's best used if your readers could be baffled by quotations from books written in non-American English, or by outmoded spellings or phrasings. For example, some readers might be puzzled by the English spelling of *emphasise* and assume that the writer made a mistake. *Sic* could be useful in this case.

✓ Bertie says, "you will be aware that I have frequently had occasion to emphasise [*sic*] the fact that Aunt Dahlia is all right."

QUOTATION MARKS

TITLES

Use quotation marks around titles of short works: essays, short stories, newspaper and magazine articles, songs, poems, chapter titles, and TV show episodes.

✓ Chester did an interpretive dance to "Toxic."

✓ Ursula recited Elizabeth Bishop's poem "The Moose."

DIALOGUE

Surround direct quotations with double quotation marks. A change of speaker is usually indicated with a new paragraph. For more, see QUOTATIONS.

✓ "I thought you owned the Barbie Dream House."
"Sadly, no. My parents refuse to buy it for me."

You don't necessarily have to change paragraphs each time the speaker switches. If you decide to cover a conversation in one paragraph, be sure to identify who's speaking so your readers don't get confused.

✓ "I thought you owned the Barbie Dream House," said Jeanette. "What planet do you live on?" scoffed Mark. "My parents refuse to buy it for me."

Do not use quotation marks unless you are quoting direct speech.

✓ Please don't say no until you hear me out.

Similarly, do not use quotation marks if you are explaining what someone said without actually quoting her.

✓ Georgia told Bill she felt sick and had to leave.

THOUGHTS

You can surround thoughts with quotation marks or not, according to your preference.

✓ "My heart is filled with bile," thought Aoife.
✓ My heart is filled with bile, thought Aoife.

DEFINITIONS AND TRANSLATIONS

You can use quotation marks to indicate a translation of a non-English word.

✓ The kids often call Mr. Quigley *un tostón insoportable*, "a real pain."

NICKNAMES

If you want to mention someone's nickname within his or her name, put the nickname in quotes.

✓ Adam "The Hammer" Feinman narrowed his eyes.

DISTANCING EFFECT

Quotation marks can be used to suggest that you're using a word ironically or in an unusual way. When used this way, quotation marks are called *scare quotes*. Try to use scare quotes as little as possible. They almost always make you sound condescending and snotty.

✓ You call it preproduction; ad guys like us call it "prepro."
✓ With a snarl, the waitress plopped the "food" down on the table.

SLANG

There is no need to enclose familiar slang words or expressions in quotation marks.

✓ Myra longed for some bling-bling of her own.

If you think your readers will be completely baffled by a particular slang word or expression, you might want to enclose it in quotation marks.

✓ Grant called our attention to the beautiful "dimes" walking down the street.

QUOTATION vs. QUOTE

quotation: a passage or line (*n.*)

✓ Melissa picked a particularly raunchy quotation from *Much Ado About Nothing*.

quote: to repeat another's words (*v.*)

✓ To impress her audience, Melissa planned to quote Shakespeare.

REDUNDANCIES

Avoid redundancies like *in my own personal opinion* (if you say *my own*, we already know it's your *personal* opinion). Such phrases make your writing sound flabby and boring, and should be mercilessly cut. Below is a list of some common redundant phrases:

audible sound	refer back
biography of his life	revert back
close proximity	the reason . . . is because
completely unanimous	the reason why . . . is because
each and every	six a.m. in the morning
end result	six p.m. at night
the future to come	small in size
if and when	true fact
in actual fact	twelve midnight
one and the same	twelve noon
return again	

RHETORICAL QUESTIONS

A *rhetorical question* expects no answer—it's used for *rhetorical* effect.

At best, rhetorical questions are pompous. At worst, they are a transparent attempt to avoid coming to a conclusion. Avoid them in your writing.

UNDESIRABLE: But what does Beatrice really feel about Benedick?

BETTER: Despite her annoyance with Benedick, Beatrice secretly enjoys his company.

RUN-ON SENTENCES

Run-on sentence is an umbrella term that encompasses both sentences that have been joined up improperly with no punctuation and *comma splices,* which are sentences that have been joined up improperly with a comma.

RUN-ON: The haunted house is especially scary this year little kids might not want to come.

COMMA SPLICE: Sharon desperately wanted to make the hockey team, she practiced for hours every day.

COMMA SPLICE: We considered going to the football game, however, in the end we decided it was too cold outside.

There are a few ways to fix run ons and comma splices. One of the simplest methods is to use a semicolon between the two independent clauses.

✓ The haunted house is especially scary this year; little kids might not want to come.

✓ Sharon desperately wanted to make the hockey team; she practiced for hours every day.

You can also fix comma splices by adding a conjunction after the comma.

✓ Sharon desperately wanted to make the hockey team, and she practiced for hours every day.

Finally, you can fix comma splices by making one clause subordinate to the other—which is a fancy way of saying you can fix the problem by making the relationship between the two clauses more clear.

✓ Although we considered going to the football game, in the end we decided it was too cold outside.

You might notice that comma splices are rampant in respected newspapers, celebrated novels, and so on.

✓ He was brash, he was arrogant, he was utterly charming.

✓ It's not you, it's me.

If you're a talented writer who has a firm grasp on grammar, you might want to use comma splices occasionally for dramatic effect. In general, though, comma splices should be avoided.

SEMICOLONS

Semicolons are used to connect two related independent clauses.

✓ One minute, Clarence was doing the electric slide; the next minute, he was sulking in the corner.

A semicolon must be used before these adverbs if they separate independent clauses: *besides, however, indeed, then, therefore*.

✓ That tinsel costs too much; besides, it looks tacky.

✓ Sly planned on asking Rachel to the dance; however, he chickened out at the last minute.

✓ Your outfit is shocking; indeed, it's the least fashionable ensemble I've ever seen.

Use a semicolon before *that is, for example*, and similar expressions to avoid run-on sentences.

RUN-ON: Our mothers agreed, that is, they caved in after we whined and complained for weeks.

✓ Our mothers agreed; that is, they caved in after we whined and complained for weeks.

LISTS WITH COMMAS

If items in a list are clauses that are punctuated with commas, separate the clauses with semicolons.

✓ Nanette despairingly considered her red heels, which had a hole in the toe; her ballet flats, which were tattered; and her clogs, which gave her terrible blisters.

If items in a list are groups that are punctuated with commas, you should separate the groups with semicolons.

✓ Laura has it all: brains, wit, and courage; sparkling dark eyes, long brown limbs, and a mane of chestnut hair; and glittering prospects.

LISTS WITH LENGTHY ITEMS

For clarity, you may also choose to separate lengthy items with semicolons.

✓ Cherry slowly realized that her air conditioner was broken beyond repair; that her sole fan was stored thousands of miles away in the farthest reaches of her parents' basement; and that the weather forecast was for intense humidity and temperatures in the mid-nineties.

SENTENCE STRUCTURE

In order to avoid boring your readers to death, vary your sentence structure.

UNDESIRABLE: Her husband does not allow her to work. He does not allow her to take care of her baby. She longs to do something other than rest. Everyone says she is sick and must relax. She is trapped in her room. Eventually she begins to go mad.

BETTER: Because of her purported sickness, everyone, including her husband, insists she must rest instead of working or taking care of her baby. Trapped in her room, she begins to go mad.

By varying your sentence structure, you not only keep things lively, you indicate to your readers which assertions are most important. They'll instinctively understand that subordinated details (*trapped in her room*) aren't as crucial as prominent points (*she begins to go mad*), and they'll have a much easier time understanding your writing.

SERIAL COMMA

Everyone agrees that items in a series should be separated with commas. But not everyone agrees that the last (*serial*) comma, which comes before the conjunction in a list, is necessary.

SERIAL COMMA: Today we learned about bug bites, poison ivy, and rashes.

WITHOUT SERIAL COMMA: Today we learned about bug bites, poison ivy and rashes.

We at SparkNotes are advocates of the serial comma. We think it makes prose clearer and more readable — which is, after all, the point of punctuation. And it resolves potential ambiguities in such phrases as *The author would like to thank her parents, Jesus and Mrs. Chin.*

WITH AMPERSANDS

Don't use the serial comma before ampersands.

✓ Judy, Liza & Co. sponsored the cabaret contest.

SINGULAR SUBJECTS

There are many subjects that look plural but are actually singular. Here is a list of some tricky singular nouns and pronouns:

NOUNS	PRONOUNS
America	anybody
amount	anyone
audience	each
crowd	either
a couple	everybody
family	everyone
group	neither
a number	nobody
	none
	no one
	one

Be sure to match these nouns with singular verbs, not plural verbs.

✓ Neither of them likes MTV.

✓ As her family cheers her to victory, Caitlin sets the world record in trampoline jumping.

SIGHT, SITE

See Cite, Sight, and Site.

SPLIT INFINITIVES

A split infinitive occurs when an adverb is insinuated between *to* and a verb.

SPLIT INFINITIVES: To honestly say; to bravely proclaim; to basically snub;
   to grudgingly do; to greatly worry

In the old days, split infinitives were strictly forbidden. Now, however, most people don't mind them if the alternative, more correct version sounds awkward. The classic example is Captain Kirk's famous phrase *to boldly go where no man has gone before*. To many people, *to go boldly where no man has gone before* would sound distinctly odd.

STATIONARY vs. STATIONERY

stationary: unmoving (*adj.*)
✓ Dan rarely used his stationary bike.

stationery: nice paper (*n.*)
✓ Dan wrote thank-you letters on Mickey Mouse stationery.

The *e* in stationery is for *envelope*.

SUBJECT-VERB AGREEMENT

EITHER . . . OR, NEITHER . . . NOR
If you have two singular subjects joined by an *either . . . or* or *neither . . . nor* expression, use a singular verb. This is also true for two singular subjects joined by *or*.
✓ Neither Henrietta nor Guy is skilled at dodgeball.
✓ Luke or Ian was responsible for the outrageous chicken prank.

If you have one singular subject and one plural subject joined by *either . . . or* or *neither . . . nor,* match the verb to the subject closest to it.

✓ Either the ghosts or the headless horseman is sure to terrify the kids.

✓ Either the headless horseman or the ghosts are sure to terrify the kids.

AS WELL AS

Don't be tricked by phrases like *as well as, along with, in addition to,* and so on. Their presence does not mean you should match a singular subject with a plural verb.

✓ Sudha, along with the rest of the ballet class, hates pink tutus.

TRICKY SINGULAR NOUNS

Many nouns that look plural are actually singular. For more on this, see SINGULAR SUBJECTS.

TAKE

See BRING VS. TAKE.

TENSE

When narrating and summarizing, keep your tenses straight. In the example below, the writer begins by describing what Demi recalls. The writer's subsequent switch into the past tense is fine (the concert happened in the past), but the switch back to the present tense is not fine.

SHIFTING TENSE: In the second chapter, Demi recalls attending the concert to see her best friend perform. At first she found the event slow and tedious, but eventually she gets interested and stops feeling so sleepy.

Remember, shifting between different tenses is fine as long as each shift is logical and done on purpose.

THAN vs. THEN

Many people use *than* when they mean *then*, and vice versa.

Than, a conjunction, is used to compare things.

Then, an adverb, is used with descriptions of time.

✓ Then, suddenly, Mr. Perez shouted, "I'm a better diver than you'll ever be!"

✓ I think she looks dangerously skinny, but then, what do I know?

THAT vs. WHICH

In general, *which* is used to introduce *nonrestrictive phrases*. If you take out a nonrestrictive phrase, the sentence should still make sense and have the same meaning.

✓ This ugly leopard-print chair, which haunts my nightmares, is my husband's.

If you take out *which haunts my nightmares*, the sentences still retains its meaning: *This ugly leopard-print chair is my husband's.*

That is used to introduce *restrictive phrases*. A restrictive phrase is essential to the meaning of the sentence.

✓ The chair that looks as though a leopard died on top of it is my husband's.

If you take out the phrase *that looks as though a leopard died on top of it*, then the resulting stub (*The chair is my husband's*) no longer identifies the chair properly. The phrase *that looks as though a leopard died on top of it* restricts the field of all possible chairs to identify the particular chair the speaker has in mind.

If you're struggling to decide whether *which* or *that* is correct, remember this basic rule: if you see commas, use *which*. If you don't, use *that*.

✓ The green coat that you tossed on the floor is vintage Valentino.

✓ This coat, which you treated so casually, is worth thousands of dollars.

When discussing people rather than things, use *who* or *whom* instead of *which* and *that*. See WHO VS. WHOM for more on the difference.

It's okay to use *that* to refer to people, but *which* only works for things.

✓ The nurses that eat lunch at Subway wear purple scrubs.

✓ The lunching nurses, who sat at the corner table, sadly decided that they couldn't get away with wearing orange socks.

THEIR, THERE, AND THEY'RE

Mixing up *their*, *there*, and *they're* is an easy way to make yourself look silly.

Their is a possessive pronoun.

There refers to location.

They're is a contraction of *they are*.

✓ Their love of golf baffles me.

✓ There they are, heading to the green in their golf cart.

✓ They're terrible players, but that doesn't stop them.

Be careful not to confuse *theirs* with *there's*. And whatever you do, don't use *their's* at all.

Theirs is a possessive pronoun.

There's is a contraction of *there is*.

✓ Is this foot-long sub ours or theirs?

✓ There's no excuse for stealing their pickles.

THIS AND THAT

Don't start sentences with words like *this* or *that* and expect the reader to figure out what you're referring to. Instead, elaborate on *this* or *that*, or avoid starting sentences with them altogether.

AMBIGUOUS: The embittered gym teacher explained that the talent contest had been rigged and that Danielle's victory was always assured. This enraged Greta.

CLEAR: The embittered gym teacher explained that the talent contest had been rigged and that Danielle's victory was always assured. This evidence of the school's corruption enraged Greta.

CLEAR: The embittered gym teacher explained that the talent contest had been rigged and that Danielle's victory was always assured. The news of Danielle's unfair win enraged Greta.

TITLES OF WORKS

ITALICS VS. QUOTATION MARKS

Italicize the titles of novels, books, movies, long poems, plays, CDs, and TV series, and the names of newspapers, magazines, and journals.

✓ The *Washington Post* reviewer looked ashen after seeing the world's worst production of *The Phantom of the Opera*.

Put quotation marks around the titles of chapters, episodes of TV shows, essays, articles, photographs, poems, short stories, and songs.

✓ Every Halloween, Ming sings "Monster Mash" as she decorates her room with orange and black streamers.

CAPITALIZATION

There are no firm rules governing capitalization, but there are some traditions.

Lowercase short prepositions—as long as they're not a crucial part of the title or used as adverbs, adjectives, or conjunctions.

✓ Christiane listened to "Stand by Me" on the way to see *Up the Down Staircase*.

Lowercase *and*, *as*, *but*, *for*, *or*, *nor*, and *to*.

✓ You may be surprised to learn that the actual title begins *The Life and Strange Surprizing Adventures of Robinson Crusoe, of York, Mariner*—and the subtitle goes on from there.

Lowercase *a*, *an*, and *the*.

✓ "All on a Golden Afternoon" is my favorite Disney song, next to "I'm Waiting for the One I Love."

The rule that trumps all others: always capitalize the first and last words of titles. This means that if a title ends in *the*, for example, or begins in *up*, you must capitalize those words.

✓ Rosie is reading *The Thing That Slimed Me*.
✓ Christian wrote the article called "Hard to Talk To."

NEWSPAPERS AND MAGAZINES

Even if the names of newspapers and magazines officially begin with *the* or another article, don't italicize or capitalize that article.

✓ As soon as the *New Yorker* arrived, Anna devoured Anthony Lane's review of the movie.

Don't italicize or capitalize words like *newspaper* or *magazine* unless they are actually part of a newspaper or magazine's title.

✓ I enjoy the gossipy pages of *Us Weekly* magazine.

SINGULAR

Note that titles always take a singular verb, even if they mention plural items.

✓ *Jumpers* isn't Sarah's first choice, but she'll see it if *Bug* is sold out.

TIME

MONTHS AND DAYS

The days of the week and months of the year should always be capitaized in text.

✓ On Thursday afternoons, Judith mows the Patterson-Smiths' enormous lawn.

✓ Eight Januaries ago, a little boy was born in Cook County hospital.

In text, write out the words in full. Elsewhere, they may be abbreviated.

Monday	Mon.
Tuesday	Tues., Tue.
Wednesday	Wed.
Thursday	Thurs., Thur.
Friday	Fri.
Saturday	Sat.
Sunday	Sun.
January	Jan.
February	Feb.
March	Mar.
April	Apr.
May	May
June	Jun., June
July	Jul., July

August	Aug.
September	Sept., Sep.
October	Oct.
November	Nov.
December	Dec.

ERAS

See the entries on A.D. and B.C.

TIMES OF THE DAY

| ante meridiem (before noon) | a.m. |
| post meridiem (after noon) | p.m. |

You can abbreviate *ante meridiem* and *post meridiem* either with lower-case letters and periods (*a.m.*, *p.m.*) or with small caps (AM, PM).

If you use *a.m.* or *p.m.*, saying *in the morning* or *in the evening* is redundant.

✓ Let's meet at Bowlmor at 11 p.m.

✓ Let's meet at Bowlmor at eleven in the evening.

TORTUOUS vs. TORTUROUS

tortuous: twisting

✓ Andy felt that the unfamiliar hallways were a tortuous maze.

torturous: torture-related

✓ Andy's first encounter with the popular kids was particularly torturous.

TRANSITIONAL SENTENCES

Transitions are the sentences or words that allow readers to follow the flow of your argument. A well-placed transition will take your reader gently by the hand and shepherd him along. In the examples below, transitional words and phrases are italicized for clarity only.

ELABORATING

Transitions can alert your reader that you are about to elaborate on a point.

✓ Paul pirouettes as if he's drunk. *Furthermore*, his leaps are pathetically low to the ground.

PROVIDING AN EXAMPLE

Use transitions to show that you're going to provide examples.

✓ Tammy is a very picky eater. *For example*, last year she ate nothing but steak tartare, creamed spinach, and blueberries.

SHOWING CONTRAST

Transitions can be used to show contrast.

✓ Manzur worships Dolly Parton. Biff, *on the other hand*, hates country music in general and Dolly Parton in particular.

SHOWING RESULTS

Transitions can be used to indicate results.

✓ You spend most of your work hours chatting on the phone. *Therefore*, I have no choice but to fire you.

SHOWING SEQUENCE

Use transitions to show sequences of events.

✓ *At first*, Tia wanted to be a model. *Soon after* moving to L.A., she decided acting was her true passion. *Eventually*, she ditched acting and took up photography.

UNDERLINING

Underlining can serve the same function as italicizing. You can underline book titles, emphasized words, and so on; it's a handy way to work when hand-writing text. But italicizing is preferable to underlining.

ACCEPTABLE: <u>Uncle John's Bathroom Reader</u> is my favorite book.

DESIRABLE: *Uncle John's Bathroom Reader* is my favorite book.

Whatever you do, be consistent. If you choose to italicize (which you should), don't underline at all; if you choose to underline (which you shouldn't), don't italicize at all.

UNINTERESTED

See DISINTERESTED VS. UNINTERESTED.

VERBING NOUNS

Some nouns gradually become verbs. Verbing—using a noun as a verb—nouns has a long history in the English language, but some people are enraged to see words they've always considered nouns and nouns alone used as verbs. Therefore, tread lightly.

DANGEROUS: The producers greenlighted Ted's script.

SAFE: The producers gave Ted's script the green light.

VERBS, IRREGULAR

Lie and *lay* are two notoriously difficult verbs; people often get them mixed up in the past tense. For more, see LAY VS. LIE. Here are some other verbs that can get tricky in the past tense:

PRESENT	SIMPLE PAST	PAST PARTICIPLE
arise	arose	arisen
become	became	become
begin	began	begun
blow	blew	blown
break	broke	broken
choose	chose	chosen
come	came	come
dive	dived, dove	dived
do	did	done
draw	drew	drawn
drink	drank	drunk

PRESENT	SIMPLE PAST	PAST PARTICIPLE
drive	drove	driven
drown	drowned	drowned
dwell	dwelled	dwelled
eat	ate	eaten
fall	fell	fallen
fight	fought	fought
flee	fled	fled
fling	flung	flung
fly	flew	flown
forget	forgot	forgotten
freeze	froze	frozen
get	got	gotten
give	gave	given
go	went	gone
grow	grew	grown
hang (a thing)	hung	hung
hang (a person)	hanged	hanged
know	knew	known
lay	laid	laid
lead	led	led
lie (recline)	lay	lain
lie (tell fibs)	lied	lied
plead	pleaded	pleaded
put	put	put
ride	rode	ridden
ring	rang	rung
rise	rose	risen
run	ran	run
see	saw	seen
set	set	set
shine (give light)	shone	shone

PRESENT	SIMPLE PAST	PAST PARTICIPLE
shine (make shiny)	shined	shined
shake	shook	shaken
shrink	shrank	shrunk
shut	shut	shut
sing	sang	sung
sink	sank	sunk
sit	sat	sat
speak	spoke	spoken
spring	sprang	sprung
sting	stung	stung
strive	strove, strived	striven, strived
swear	swore	sworn
swim	swam	swum
swing	swang	swung
take	took	taken
tear	tore	torn
throw	threw	thrown
wake	woke, waked	woken, waked
wear	wore	worn
write	wrote	written

VOICE

Writing teachers often talk about "finding your voice." Whether you are writing status reports, term papers, or letters, it is important to find a voice that is lively and engaging, and not stuffy or grating.

STUFFY: Egg's overwrought enthusiasm and plethora of literary references are overwhelming. Egg profusely quotes Jefferson and Volny in order to illustrate the fact that the triumph of "humane and free" modernity rests on the remains of subjugated multitudes.

BETTER: The combination of Egg's enthusiasm and his frequent literary references can be a little overwhelming. He agrees that "humane and free" modernity can only exist when people are subjugated, and turns to Jefferson and Volny to lend this idea authority.

GRATING: On many—many!—occasions, Hamlet practically goes ahead and accuses his mother of being a slut. He doesn't have any evidence for this, so . . . what is he talking about?

BETTER: On many occasions, Hamlet practically accuses his mother of sleeping around. The evidence for this assertion is scanty.

See also ACTIVE VOICE.

WELL

See GOOD VS. WELL.

WHICH

See THAT VS. WHICH.

WHO VS. WHOM

Who is a subject pronoun; it is used as the subject of a verb. *Whom* is an object pronoun; it is never used as the subject of a verb.

✓ Jacqueline, whom you may remember from high school, is now a *Jeopardy* champion.

If you can't get *who* and *whom* straight, try this trick: rephrase the sentence to get rid of *who* or *whom*. If you find you've replaced *who/whom* with *he, she,* or *they, who* is correct. If you find you've replaced *who/whom* with *him, her,* or *them,* then *whom* is correct.

For example, suppose you have the question *Who/whom is the most famous A-list star eating lunch at Elaine's?* Rephrase it: *She is the most famous A-list star eating lunch at Elaine's.* Since you've used *she,* you know *who* is correct in the original question: *Who is the most famous A-list star at Elaine's?*

Another example: *Vaughn wondered who/whom he would kiss next.* Rephrase: *Vaughn would kiss her next.* Since the rephrased sentence uses *her,* you know *whom* is correct: *Vaughn wondered whom he would kiss next.*

WHO'S vs. WHOSE

who's: contraction of *who is*

✓ Who's the nitwit in the SUV?

whose: belonging to someone (*possessive adj.*)

✓ Whose tiny convertible is parked in the fire lane?

WORDINESS

Being wordy doesn't mean writing long, complex sentences; long, complex sentences are perfectly acceptable. Being wordy means failing to use only the words you absolutely need, and no more. Wordiness is often a sign of pretentiousness or an attempt to sound official. If you see phrases like *being that* or *in regards to the fact that,* you know you're dealing with a writer who's not nearly as smart as she thinks she is.

These undesirable phrases are italicized in the examples below.

WORDY: This atrocious children's book explains the mystery *as to* why dogs bark.

BETTER: This atrocious children's book explains the mystery of why dogs bark.

WORDY: *Being that* you ate the last maraschino cherry, you should buy a new jar.

BETTER: Because you ate the last maraschino cherry, you should buy a new jar.

WORDY: *Due to the fact that* she made a spectacular save in the fourth quarter, Min was named MVP.

BETTER: As a result of her spectacular save in the fourth quarter, Min was named MVP.

WORDY: *In the event* that the fire alarm sounds, run screaming from the building.

BETTER: If the fire alarm sounds, run screaming from the building.

WORDY: The memo *in regards to* orange wipes was circulated throughout the office.

BETTER: The memo about orange wipes was circulated throughout the office.

WORDY: *The reason why* Barbie's hair is ruined *is that* I gave her a bath.

BETTER: Barbie's hair is ruined because I gave her a bath.

WORDY: I *was unaware of the fact that* Christopher lost his boots.

BETTER: I didn't know that Christopher lost his boots.

WORDY: Henry will be out tomorrow *owing to the fact* that he has chicken pox.

BETTER: Henry will be out tomorrow because he has chicken pox.

Wordiness is often the last refuge of terrified students trying to write five-page papers in three hours. "Maybe if I just babble on for a while, inserting fancy phrases willy-nilly," the thinking goes, "my professor will be impressed." On the contrary! Your professors will see right through you, and your pompous wordiness will only annoy them.

YOU'RE vs. YOUR

You're is a contraction meaning "you are," and *your* is a possessive pronoun.

✓ You're not going to wear your miniskirt in this snowstorm, are you? Your knees will freeze!

LIST OF ENTRIES

Accents
Accept vs. Except
Active Voice
A.D.
Addresses
Adjectives
Adverbs
Adverse vs. Averse
Affect vs. Effect
Afterward vs. Afterword
Aggravate vs. Irritate
All Ready vs. Already
All Together vs. Altogether
Allude vs. Elude
Allusion vs. Illusion
Altar vs. Alter
And, But, and Because
Any One vs. Anyone
Any Way vs. Anyway
A Part vs. Apart
Apostrophes
Appositives
As
Averse
A While vs. Awhile
Bad vs. Badly
B.C.
Because
Bibliography
Born vs. Borne
Brackets
Brand Names
Bring vs. Take
Briticisms
But
Capitalization
Capital vs. Capitol
Cardinal Numbers
Censor vs. Censure
Citations in Text
Cite, Sight, and Site
Claims, Inflated
Clichés
Colloquial Expressions

Colons
Commas
Complement vs. Compliment
Compound Words
Conditional
Confidant(e) vs. Confident
Conjunctions
Contractions
Cultural Terms
Dashes
Dates
Deduce vs. Induce
Definite vs. Definitive
Defuse vs. Diffuse
Desert vs. Dessert
Dialogue
Diffuse
Directions
Discreet vs. Discrete
Disinterested vs. Uninterested
Double Negatives
Each Other vs. One Another
Effect
Either . . . Or, Neither . . . Nor
E.G. vs. I.E.
Elicit vs. Illicit
Ellipses
Elude
Emigrate vs. Immigrate
Endnotes
Et Al.
Et Cetera, Etc.
Every Day vs. Everyday
Every One vs. Everyone
Except
Exclamation Points
Fancy Words
Farther vs. Further
Faze vs. Phase
Faulty Comparisons
Fewer
Figures of Speech
Flare vs. Flair
Footnotes and Endnotes

Former vs. Latter
Fragments
Further
Gendered Language
Gerunds
Good vs. Well
Historical Terms
Hyphens
Ibid.
I.E.
Illicit
Illusion
Immigrate
Imply vs. Infer
Induce
Infer
–ing Words
Interjections
Irritate
Italics
It's vs. Its
I vs. Me
Jargon
Latter
Lay vs. Lie
Less vs. Fewer
Lie
Like vs. As
Lists
Loath vs. Loathe
Loose vs. Lose
Margins
May Be vs. Maybe
Me
Military Terms
Misplaced Modifiers
Misused Words
Mixed Metaphors
Moral vs. Morale
Names and Titles
Nauseous vs. Nauseated
Neither . . . Nor
Nonexistent Words
Numbers

One Another
Opinions
Ordinal Numbers
Parallel Structure
Parentheses
Passive Voice
Peak vs. Pique
Periods
Phase
Pique
Place Names
Plurals
Political Terms
Pore vs. Pour
Prepositions
Pronouns
Prophesy vs. Prophecy
Proscribe vs. Prescribe
Qualifiers

Question Marks
Quotations
Quotation Marks
Quotation vs. Quote
Redundancies
Rhetorical Questions
Run-on Sentences
Semicolons
Sentence Structure
Serial Comma
Singular Subjects
Sight, Site
Split Infinitives
Stationary vs. Stationery
Subject-Verb Agreement
Superlatives
Take
Tense
Than vs. Then

That vs. Which
Their, There, and They're
This and That
Titles of Works
Time
Tortuous vs. Torturous
Transitional Sentences
Underlining
Uninterested
Verbing Nouns
Verbs, Irregular
Voice
Well
Which
Who vs. Whom
Who's vs. Whose
Wordiness
You're vs. Your